CROW CARRYING COMPANY LTD

Preface

This book is intended as a tribute to all the staff and drivers of Crow Carrying Company Ltd.

I am a former tanker driver of Tankfreight and various other tanker delivery companies. My father worked as a driver for Crow Carrying Company for 21 years and I went out with him every time I got the chance.

After my father retired I started to collect information, photographs and memorabilia on Crow Carrying Company.

This is my collection and some of the stories from the Crow Carrying drivers.

Endorsed
by Simon Crow & Malcolm Crow

Contents

History of Crow Carrying Co Ltd
Crow Drivers profiles
Crow on Contract
Crow Miscellaneous
Crow Signs & Adverts
Crow Gallery
Crow Fleet List & References
Crow Letter Heads
The End & Crow Logos

Motor Haulage Contractors

Harts Lane, North Street, Barking

With Compliments

Herbert H Crow

INTRODUCTION TO CROW CARRYING COMPANY LTD 1920

The founder of Crow Carrying Company was Mr. Latimer Crow, formerly an industrial chemist, working on projects to fill cracks in the roads and flat roof buildings. This was around the early 1920s. Latimer Crow had two sons, Herbert, who took on the responsibility of running the transport side and Fred, who continued in his father's old business. All of them were Quakers.

They first experimented in transporting hot liquids by using a 45 gallon barrel then placing it on an old horse drawn milk float. In order to keep the products hot, they covered the barrels with straw.

After a while motorisation became popular and small lorries were needed to carry this product; thus the formation of Crow Carrying Company Ltd, which was eventually built into the largest privately owned company in the country before and after World War II.

Photos below are from the Crow Carrying Co 40th Anniversary booklet except the horse and cart

Mr Latimer Crow our founder
1920-1932

Mr Herbert Crow M.D
1920-1960

Reconstruction photo of Crow Carrying Company Ltd carrying the first hot liquid product

Crow Carrying Co Ltd Story 1920-1960

Mr. Latimer Crow was active in the business until shortly before his death in 1932, at the age of 77 years. From commencement, his younger son Herbert, who later became Chairman and Managing Director, worked with his father. Mr. F. J. Reynolds joined the company a few months later eventually becoming Director in charge of Operations and Maintenance. Other Directors were Mr. F. Rowland Waller, FCA, and Mr. Fred. B. Crow, the Company Secretary was Mr. Harry L Pedley FCA.

Photos from the 40th anniversary of Crow Carrying Co booklet

Original Offices 1920

Main Garage 1925

Mr F. J. Reynolds, M. Inst. T., M.I.E.C
1920-1960

Crow's Offices 1932

Crow Carrying Co Ltd Story 1920-1960

The fleet of Crow Carrying Company not only grew numerically, but also in vehicle size. From the first tanker of 800 gallon capacity, this was surpassed by 1000, 1250, 1500 and on to 3,800 and 4,000 gallons in five compartments for the carriage of petrol. Under Home Office regulations, 1947 could have proved a critical year for the firm with the nationalisation of Road Haulage, but its service was by then so specialised that it was excluded. It is only experience over many years that can give the practical knowledge so essential in a field that must be pioneered with each new development. Alongside the operational experience, and definitely complementary to it, was the efficient fleet maintenance. This was grown under the direct supervision of Mr. F. J. Reynolds. Only those who rely on a service that must not let them down can appreciate just how efficiently it ran.

As Crow Carrying Co Ltd lorries grew through the years

AEC fleet unkown 800 gallon tank   Photo courtesy of Brian Thackray collection

AEC Monarch fleet C107 with Butterfiled tank   Photo courtesy of pm photography

Crow Carrying Co Ltd 1920-1960

The motto of the Company, incorporated its Trade Mark, was "As the Crow Flies ", and as over the years, the Crow had flown and grown, the business was a far cry from that carried by the three vehicles with which it commenced. In earlier
stories of its development annual mileages were referred to in terms associated with circumnavigating our globe. It is fitting in this modern age of space travel that the mileage was over 4,000.000 per annum The total number of vehicles at that time was 185.

Scammell.Highwayman C70 1957   **Photo courtesy of pm photography**

Scammell Highwayman C10   **Photo courtesy of pm photography**

Crow Carrying Co Ltd 1920 - 1960

The new administration block was a far cry from the original office. With the post-war growth of the business, it was essential to provide more adequate maintenance, office and garage accommodation. The workshop, opened in 1951 was 250 feet long by 50 feet wide.
This was followed in October 1952 by the handsome administration block backed by a Bellman Hangar garage which had a floor area of 19,000 square feet. The completion of what was a 5-year building plan was achieved in May 1956 by the addition of two garages each 200 feet long by 90 feet wide (36,000 square feet) and an attractively designed filling station

Photo below courtesy of the 40th year Anniversary Crow Carrying Co booklet

Administrative Buidings. 1952

Filling Station . 1952   Photo courtesy of Leyland Journal

Scammell Shed. 1956   Photo courtesy of Terry Edwards collection

Crow Carrying Co Ltd 1920 -1960

Through the years the name Crow Carrying Company Ltd became well known over a wide area and work was undertaken in many parts of the country. Numerous enquiries came from the Manchester district and connections were built up.

During the second world war, vehicles on contract were stationed in Manchester and with the growth of this traffic in 1949, a small depot was opened with Mr. J A Mumford in charge. Having outgrown this accommodation, a freehold site of about 2.25 acres was acquired at Greengate, Middletown, complete with substantial buildings.

Improvements were carried out including a new office, workshop and petrol filling station. Considerable use was made through the years of the private siding facilities where rail tank- wagons containing a variety of products from the Continent, via the Harwich-Zeebrugge train ferry, were received for distribution by Road Tank Wagon.

Oldham Depot 1940s   Photos courtesy of Tom Lords collection

Photos from the 40th anniversary of Crow Carrying Co booklet

Rail Tank Wagons sidings

6

Crow Carrying Co Ltd 1920 - 1960

The company was very fortunate with their drivers, not only for their good standard of driving but in the company to customer relationship, for in truth they were the ambassadors of the firm in so many respects. In 1934 the Company entered the Safe Driving Competition of the Royal Society for the Prevention of Accidents. The driving records of its drivers then showed some twenty-five year brooches, 2 twenty-year brooches, 9 fifteen-year brooches, 17 ten-year medals and 37 five-year medals. One-hundred and nine in the Lorry Driver of the Year Competition Elimination Contest at Slough. Crow Carrying Company drivers had in their classes secured 1st and 3rd in 1956, 1st and 2nd in 1958 and a 2nd in 1959 and in addition won the cup for the best maintained vehicle for three consecutive years.

Top left.Mrs. H.H. Crow Presenting a Gold Watch to Mr. C.Squibb in Recoginition of 25 Years Service
Bottom left Mr. Howard-Hodges Addressing The Guests Before Presenting The Safe Driving Awards.
Top right. Mr. F. Wheeler Receiving Bar to 20 Year Broach
Bottom Right. Mr W. Cannon Receiving his 20 Tear Broach

Photos from the 40th anniversary of Crow Carrying Co booklet

Photo courtesy of John Smith

Driver of the year Scammell C120 John Smith

Crow Carrying Co Ltd 1920 - 1960

The post-war introduction of the drive on drive off Tilbury-Antwerp Ferry, had opened up the door to door services between this country and Europe. In furtherance of their policy of providing facilities of benefit to customers they developed this service.

Throughout its development the company maintained the family business atmosphere and had cordial relations between management and workers, which not even the General Strike of 1926 or the post-war unrest could in anyway break. A pleasing feature of the firm was the anniversary social gathering of Directorate, staff and workers which took place every year except when circumstances beyond their control intervened. The tone of these gatherings was set by the

founder who always addressed them as fellow workers and friends.

Photos from the 40th anniversary of Crow Carrying Co booklet

DIRECTORS AND STAFF WITH OVER 25 YEARS SERVICE, 1960-AGGREGATE SERVICE 434YEARS
Cyril Squibb, Jack Threshie, Ted Sams, Ben Tiller, Bill Cannon, Alf Tucker, Ted Staple, Albert Massey
Seated   Ernie Piper, David Doe, F.Reynolds, M.D H.Crow Owner Bill Wheeler, Bill Moore

Atkinson C189 on the Drive on drive off Tilbury-Antwerp Ferry

Photo courtesy of Stilltime Collection

Herbert H.Crow Story 1920 -1960

Herbert Crow enjoyed his job so much it was like a hobby to him. Since his father, Latimer Crow started the firm in 1920, the Crow family had deep roots in West Ham and the surrounding area.

Almost 100+ years ago they established there as tar distillers. Herbert was born into the Christian way of life, which was rigidly upheld. His grandfather was very much the head of the family. Herbert Crow remembered the day when one of his uncles remarked "surely father I am to make my own choices in life", it was made very clear that he wasn't.

Thus it was that the formative years of Herbert Crow's adolescence were spent between a typical Victorian home and the comparative freedom of the City of London School. Never very strong physically, he was not required to play games, in which he lacked interest. Instead, he devoted himself to the school rambling and debating societies and acted as editor of the publications of these institutions. It is clearly from those days that he gained his fondness for debate and public speaking.

Destined to join the family business, Herbert was sent for two years to the tar works of the South Metropolitan Gas Co. and then returned to his father, Latimer Crow, at the West Ham plant, of which he was ultimately Works Manager. During the first World War (1914-18), he never reached the standard of fitness required by the Services. With the Armistice, some contraction of the tar business was inevitable. As the West Ham plant closed production then concentrated on the second works at Barking. Herbert Crow's father and uncle retired and the business was then directed by a cousin, ,in 1920, merged with a similar distilling enterprise at Rotherhithe. Herbert went with the new company, but felt unhappy about it and, perhaps to his relief, was dismissed in 1920. A year of retirement was enough for his father. Looking around for some fresh field in which to exploit his talents, he bought three lorries, founded Crow Carrying Company Ltd., with a capital of £7,000, and entered the haulage business with a useful contract for carrying canned petrol. The vehicles were parked overnight next door to the Barking tar works and young Herbert helped out by doing the paper work when his distilling days were over. With the fall of the amalgamation axe, he had a job to go to.

Photo courtesy of Barking Libary Archive

The Crow Family Business

Crow's first lorry Thornycroft 1920

Photo courtesy of Ian Allan Libary

The Herbert H. Crow Story 1920 - 1960

The years up to the outbreak of World War II were time of steady hard work. The haulage business grew, although not without difficulty. Each year, three more lorries would be added to the fleet and it was largely Herbert Crow who found the work for them. Contracts led to other contracts, but there were also disappointments. Shortly before World War II the founder of the business died, just at a time when the tide had turned for the company. It was of regret to the Chairman that his father didn't see the business as it was then. The company went on to operate 182 bulk liquid tankers, about half being on Contract-A licence. The capital value of the company grew to £225,000 and the Barking headquarters, built in 1951, comprised of well-appointed offices, a large garage and workshop and a private wharf on the River Roding. There was also a large depot at Middleton, Manchester, serving the North.

In the mid-1960s, Herbert Crow, a tall man with a slight stoop had the definite features that were a delight to cartoonists. An excellent example hung on the wall of his office (He's a Crow, but he won't Rook you).

A fluent and entertaining speaker, Mr. Crow addressed nearly 50 rotary clubs on the subject of road haulage. He was a founder member and past President of Barking Rotary and a past President of Barking Manufacturers' Association. His membership of trade associations dated back to 1923, when he joined 'London Cartage'. He served on the committee from 1923 onwards and in a similar capacity for the Commercial Motor Users' Association in 1933-34. He joined the Road Haulage Association in 1945 and was proud of his office of National Vice-Chairman. He was also Junior Warden of the Carmen's Company and a Vice President of the Institute of Transport.

The demands of business and committee work did not allow Herbert Crow much relaxation. What leisure time he had was spent at his home at South Woodford or in his caravan in the countryside. During the years he compiled scrapbooks, largely from newspaper cuttings, of his schooldays, his family affairs and, most impressive of all, his business. Herbert Crow was a man utterly devoted to the well-being of a fine and old-established family business. Unhappily, he had no son to follow in his footsteps. It is typical of the man that the greatest part of his leisure time was occupied with the future of the industry of which he had been a leading member for nearly 40 years.

Photo courtesy of Malcolm Crow

HERBERT H. CROW   **Photo courtesy of Commercial Motor**

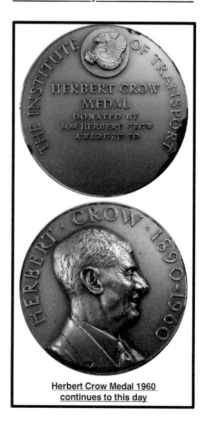

Herbert Crow Medal 1960
continues to this day

Specialists in Transporting Road Materials 1931

Local Government Highways Department were experiencing difficulties in arranging the transport of the products they required for road repairs, especially liquids . In 1920 Crow Carrying Company, founded its business and decided to specialise in this type of work. One reason for this decision was the fact that the governing director Mr. Latimer Crow, and his son Herbert, were, in former years, both closely connected with tar distillation. Crow Carrying Company was then working from Barking East London. There were then more than 36 motors in use, which included tankers, having the capacities from 300 gallons, whilst the motors could carry from 1 ton to 15 tons. The transportation of solids and liquids for road making formed a large part of the work of concern, special attention being D48 paid for the need for machines to carry dressings, etc. At a temperature considerably above atmospheric, for this duty insulated tanks were provided.

Suitable loading and unloading pumps were built into the motors.whilst tipping lorries were, of course, used for loose products. By employment of such a service it was possible for those using spraying machines to keep the appliances at work all day, without breaking off to make transporting journeys from factories or railway yards to the scene of operation. Obviously, it was not an economical proposition to use a special duties machine as a plain carrying unit. The use of a Crow transporter vehicle enabled the sprayer to dispose of 3,000 gallons to 4,000 gallons of liquid in a working day.

In addition to those for tar and similar liquids, tankers could be provided for petrol, benzene white spirit, turpentine, alcohol, fuel oils, lubricating oils and ammonia. Crow Carrying could also provide machines for edible oils. Although particular attention was paid to the needs of the gas and tar distilling industries, a range of road transport lorries were available for many other requirements. Regular services were in operation, one of the earliest started between London Northampton carrying boots and shoes.

Photo below courtesy of Ian Alan Library

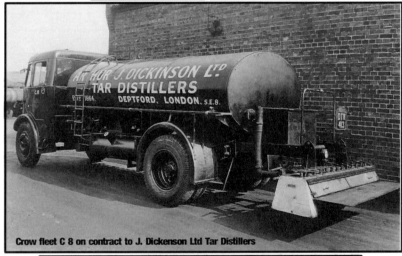

Crow fleet C 8 on contract to J. Dickenson Ltd Tar Distillers

Above One of the Leyland tanker
C30 early 1920s

Photo courtesy of Commercial Motor

Crow Carrying Co Ltd - Specialised Methods 1936

The main delivery for Crow Carrying Company Ltd was bulk liquids, but also had regular runs
between London and Northampton delivering over 20 different classes of products. Eight wheeler tankers
were among a fleet of 49 motors. A list of products they delivered covered almost every letter of the alphabet
from A to X inclusive.

The fleet then 49 motors, which included a Rolls-Royce breakdown tender, which
Mr. Herbert H Crow had his own Rolls-Royce car cut up and made into it by the fitters. When Rolls-Royce
found out they weren't very happy and wanted to buy it back. Mr. Herbert H Crow was having none of it.
The other vehicles were a Albion, Bedford, Dennis, Leyland, Morris-Commercial and Thornycroft, makes.
Crow Carrying claimed to run the biggest tanker in the country a Scammell 3,850-gallon outfit with a
Thompson Brothers stainless-steel tank body, for the movement of industrial alcohol.
Other motors included a Scammell Mechanical Horse. Crow Carrying had achieved a reputation for the
movement of liquids since 1921. The company worked a regular twice weekly service from London to
Northampton. The route was covered by a Bedford 3-ton Luton-type van and the same driver had been on it
from the start-up and until 1940s this was for the transporting of boots. Crow Carrying also took on general
haulage, transporting ice cream. The stock included insulated containers of perishables goods and
cleanliness was a top priority.

Photos courtesy of Commercial Motor except the Rolls Royce breakdown tender

Crow's Albion C49

Crow's Scammell mechanical Horse C43
Driven by Bill Moor

Two fleet Morris Commercial Vans
C41 & C42

Leyland Badger C46

AEC Monarch C38

C16 Bedford 3-ton van delivering boots

ROLLS ROYCE BREAKDOWN TENDER

1941 Crow Carrying Co Ltd Marks up 21 Years
It begins with AECs

Adherence to AEC machines over two decades was shown by the Crow Carrying Company, Barking, Essex, which recorded its 21st Anniversary in 1941

Founded in 1920, the firm included a 'Y' C type Taylor engine lorry among its first three vehicles. These were used for carrying 500 can-loads of petrol for the Gas Lighting Improvement Co. Ltd., then Re-built at one period, it ran continuously until 1933. More AECs followed, a 'Y ' type 1,000gallon tanker in 1921 with a 'Y' tepee 2,500 gallon articulated tanker with a Carrimore attachment. In 1925. Other vehicles were acquired at intervening periods. For a long-time the articulated unit ran 30,000 miles a year between Thames Haven and Cambridge.

Star AEC's in Crow Carrying fleet, at this time, totalled 54 large and small vehicles, there was a Taylor-engineered 1,000gallon tanker of rare vintage. Built for service in Russia during the Great War days, it was bought to the UK during 1926, and had run ever since averaging 13,000 miles a year. Engines and parts had been replaced, but at this time the tank was 15 years old, carrying then, as in the past, refined tar. The machine was driven by only one man Mr. E. Wheeler. He had become resolutely attached to it and had consistently rejected the offer of newer vehicles. So that no other driver should take the wheel, he arranged for it to be overhauled only when he was away on annual holiday.

The last AEC to go into service was a 'Monarch' tanker, shown at Olympia in 1935. In this case the 1,650gallon tank was so fitted that it could be quickly interchanged with certain other types. The 'Monarch' carried edible oils to provincial towns and ports.

From its inception Crow Carrying Company specialised in the bulk transport of crude and refined tar. During this time, a wide variety of liquids were handled, including petrol, kerosene, turpentine, alcohol, lubricating and light diesel oils, edible oils, sulphuric and acetic acid, ammonia and vinegar. Many of these called for different types of tanks. Those of large capacity were permanently mounted; others up to 1,000gallons were interchangeable. Nearly all loads carried were Government controlled.

The outstanding characteristic of the Crow Carrying Company was the good relationship which existed between management and employee. Many men employed in the earliest days, were still on the payroll during the 1940s. Regular staff gatherings contributed a great deal towards a spirit of loyalty and co-operation. Mr. Crow's maxim was 'One man one vehicle'. Get a good driver interested in his machine and his job, and the rest is easy. The soundness of this principle was seen in the firm's twenty-one years of successful operation.

Photo below courtesy of AEC Society

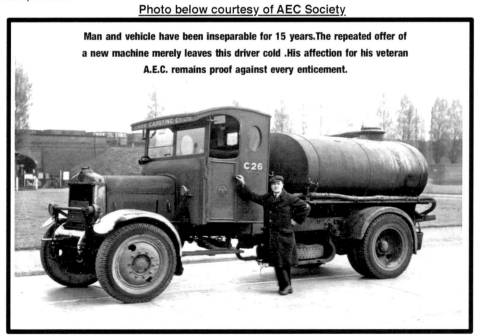

Man and vehicle have been inseparable for 15 years.The repeated offer of a new machine merely leaves this driver cold .His affection for his veteran A.E.C. remains proof against every enticement.

Deputy Mayor Visits Crow Carrying Co Ltd 1956

Twenty years prior to 1956, Crow Carrying Company Ltd, Harts Lane, Barking, opened their new workshop, thus completing the first stage of a five-year building programme. The second stage was reached in October 1952, when a new office block and garage were added. Thus saw the completion of the final and most extensive part of the building programme. The structures added being two garages and a filling station. Each garage was 200 ft. long with a span of 90 ft.—two of the largest in the country. The storage capacity of the filling station was for 5,000gallons of diesel in two 2,500gallon tanks and for 2,000gallons of petrol in a two compartment tank.

For vehicle and road tank cleaning, there was a Lay-cock two-gun high pressure washer and a Weaver steam jenny. The company ran 155 vehicles, but they were not all based at the Barking depot, which despite its size, held only half the fleet under cover.

In reply to a speech made at the opening by Mr. Herbert Crow, Chairman and Managing Director, Roy Craft, Deputy Mayor of Barking, said that, whilst he did not believe in free enterprise, if it had to be, the Crow concern was an example to follow.

The business started by Mr. Latimer Crow, father of Herbert Crow, Chairman during this time also one of the original drivers of the three vehicles then operated, was still with the company.

Photo courtesy of Transportation Magazine

Deputy Mayor inspecting under a Scammell Highwayman C103

Photo courtesy of Transportation Magazine

The completed new workshop at Crow Carrying Company 1956

Crow Carrying Co Ltd McCormack's Scammell Highwayman C127 1956

It would have been worth attending the Slough eliminating round of the Lorry Driver of the Year Competition, just to look at the Gardner engine of the Scammell tanker, driven by Mr. R. McCormack of the Crow Carrying Company Ltd. As befits a power unit with nautical traditions, it had the appearance of the engine-room of a ship made ready for an admiral's inspection. Although the vehicle had covered 52,000 miles, the under-chassis components were equally gleaming.

Mr. McCormack's tanker always looked like a new pin and he had two letters from customers to prove it. In 1955 in Coventry, he said with injured pride, "they thought I had cleaned it especially for the occasion".

Among the admirers of the vehicle was Mr. George Macaulay, from the Ministry of Works, who was a member of the National Organising committee of the competition and was invigilating at the contest.

I have heard many stories about McCormack's Scammell, one story told to me was when McCormack was out on a delivery in the C127, it started to rain so he parked it under a bridge until the rain stopped. McCormack would also clean it every chance he got.

When Mack (his nickname), got to these shows he would go up against all comers with brand new lorries and old lorries and some lorries the same age and he would beat them all.

When it came down to the Scammell being issued to someone else, that was the end of his reign. A driver called Alfie Liddard then took it over and painted over the engine bonnet cover, which ended the C127's show career.

Mr George MacAulay & McCormack having a look under the bonnet   cover of Scammell C127
Photo courtesy of Commercial Motor   Photo courtesy of Arthur Ingrham

Scammell C127 at th driver of the year 1956   Photo courtesy of NA3T Archive

Crow Carrying Co Ltd was built on Scammells

Mr. Herbert H. Crow, Chairman and Managing Director was the youngest son of the founder Mr. Latimer Crow, was there at the start of the company with his father. He was modest enough to attribute part of the company's success to the Scammell articulated vehicle. "Crow Carrying has been built on the Scammells," he said. Articulated outfits have proved absolutely right for our job from the point of view of maintenance, as well as load carrying. That being so, the Scammell which is a complete entity was a natural choice.

Scammell Coupling Gear on other Vehicles

By 1956 vehicles with Scammell couplings included 87 Scammell vehicles, all except two being tractors capable of hauling loads up to 15 tons. Scammell automatic coupling gear was also provided on other vehicles, including six Leyland Comets and two 1956 Albion FTA I ITR models. There were also eight rigid vehicles, five of them Albion's and the remainder Leyland Comets.

One of the chief benefits of articulated outfits was that trailer-tanks which were used for specific commodities and could be easily stored when they were not in use, whilst the tractor units were free to haul tankers carrying other products. Their use also permitted tankers to be loaded ready for immediate picking up by tractor unit when it completed a journey. For obvious reasons the trailer-tanks were mostly of frameless construction.

Some 20 spare tank attachments, which were interchangeable with the 15-ton tractors, were available in varying capacities for the carriage of a great variety of products. These tank carriers were produced entirely to Scammell designs drawn up to suit each type of load to be carried, and they were perfectly matched with the motive unit to provide equal weight distribution and braking coupled with the frameless form of construction, which can be said to have originated with a Scammell patent. This ensured that the vehicles were eminently suitable for their particular purpose and had maximum payload capacity.

Many of the tanks were designed for pressure-vacuum operation, and for this purpose the motive unit was fitted with the Scammell 3-cylinder radial air compressor vacuum pump which supplied air pressure up to 70 lb. psi. and vacuum for filling and discharging the load.

Bulk-liquid haulage being a highly specialised job, and Mr. Herbert Crows initial experience in the chemical industry had undoubtedly helped in the company success, thus influencing the different types of products that could be carried.

Scammell Highwayman C40 in Crow Carrying workshop   **Photo courtesy of Stilltime Collection**

Crow Carrying Co Ltd was built on Scammells

The carriage of different chemicals necessitated a further degree of segregation. Mr. Crow tells a story against himself which amply illustrates the great need for care in this direction. Some years' prior, a customer who had asked for a tanker, rang Mr. Crow to say that he had no oil to load, but would it be alright if he filled the tank with caustic soda. After a rapid thought process, Mr. Crow gave the OK. Within an hour of loading, the driver telephoned to say that the caustic soda was pouring out of the tank. Both Mr. Crow and his customer had overlooked the fact that the outlet valves of the tank were constructed of aluminium alloy to save weight, and the caustic soda had disintegrated them.

It follows then that a wide variety of materials were employed in the construction of the tanks. Whilst a mild steel tank can hold concentrated sulphuric acid, a lead lining is necessary for diluted sulphuric acid. A stainless steel tank is required for acetic acid and anhydrous acetic acids, a rubber lining for hydrochloric acid, vulcanite for sodium bisulphite, under aluminium of a purity not less than 99.5 per cent. For formaldehyde specialisation in the equipping of tanks is carried a stage further by the need for internal heat when transporting certain commodities. Hardened whale oil, vegetable oils, heavy fuel oil, glucose, bitumen, refined tar, naphthalene and glue would all be carried in insulated tanks to conserve heat.

Many of the tanks were fitted with steam coils and some with electrical elements. Certain liquids solidify, or become so viscous as to resist pumping at fairly high temperatures, and even with the best insulation a certain amount of heat is lost during a long journey. To overcome this difficulty, Scammell Lorries patented a system whereby thermostatically controlled electrical elements were fitted in the tank and used to maintain or, if necessary, raise the temperature of the load of any one tank without subjecting it to a thorough an uneconomic cleaning process. The Company's policy therefore, was to group the tanks for handling specific classes of commodity, thereby reducing both the risk of contamination and the need for complete interior cleaning between each load.

In accordance with this policy, one group of tanks were reserved for the carriage of petroleum products, another for lubricating and light diesel oils, and yet another for heavy fuel oil. Tanks for tar products were also segregated, as were those for edible oils and pharmaceutical products.

Scammell C231 at the Commercial Motor Show   Photo courtesy of Stilltime Collection

Crow Carrying Co Ltd was built on Scammells

During the course of the journey a 15 KW. generator, mounted on the tractor unit and driven from the engine crankshaft, supplied the necessary current for the heater elements as well as for a pump or other auxiliary drives that may be required. On the other hand, certain products, such as milk, have to be carried in tanks insulated so as to maintain low temperatures.

The carriage of industrial alcohol, which is subject to Customs Duty, posed scheduling problems for the company. Customs Officers have to be present when the tank is loaded and unloaded, and often the destination of a load was situated some distance away from an HM. Customs and Excise base. Incidentally, tanks carrying dutiable products were required by the Customs authorities to be secured in such a way that any tampering with the inlets and outlets was obvious. All hinge pins were spot-welded and their manholes are covered by domes, the outlet cocks being cased in. On the catches of the domes and casings there were two locks, one which can be opened only by Customs and the other by the customer.

A watch on the type and quantity of product being loaded by customers had to be kept by the company's drivers since there are striking differences in the weights of various liquids, although the problem had been largely overcome in the light of experience. For example, 3,000gallons of petroleum make up a 10-ton load, yet a 10-ton load of concentrated sulphuric acid consists of only 1,200gallons. To facilitate loading and unloading, the majority of the tanks were fitted with compressors or mechanical pumps driven by the power unit of the tractor or rigid vehicle to which they were attached.

Most of the fleet were based at the company's headquarters in Harts Lane, North Street, Barking. The only other depot being in Oldham Road, Miles Platting, Manchester, which had 28 vehicles. There were a number of vehicles out-stationed with customers, some of whom ran them in their own livery.

Vehicles working under contract invariably went to the customer new. When necessary they were replaced by further new vehicles, and after a complete overhaul and repainting were absorbed into the fleet at the Barking site. The nature of the contracts normally precluded set overhauls or major docks on a mileage basis for the majority of the vehicles, so the company relied largely on a preventive maintenance system. In the case of the vehicles based away from the depots, two fitters would be sent each month to give them a thorough check. The unit exchange system was employed at Barking, with a replacement for virtually every component always being in stock.

Maintenance and operation were the charge of another director, Mr. F. J. Reynolds, M.Inst.T., MIEC., who had also been with the company since it was founded.

The exceptionally well laid out premises at Harts Lane, included spacious workshops equipped for every contingency likely to arise in the way of repairs. The overhaul section had two pits as well as a Laycock 8-1011 vehicle hoist. Drivers entered details of suspected defects on a daily report sheet which then went to the workshops for attention. Any repair work done was entered in the record kept for each vehicle and, in addition, there was a wall chart in the engineer's office which, by means of coloured discs, gave at a glance all the major maintenance information required for every vehicle in the fleet, as well as indicating its location if it was not home based.

Photos courtesy of Leyland Journal

Crow Carrying Co Ltd was built on Scammells
Segregation of Vehicles

A 200ft. long by 95 ft. wide single span building housed the Scammell tractors and their trailer- tanks, the other vehicles in use were accommodated in an adjoining garage. This arrangement obviated confusion amongst drivers.

A kerb running the full length of the interior of the garages on each side prevented damage being caused to the tanks by backing them into the wall, this being the limit to which each driver knew he could safely reverse.

Crow Carrying practiced the one-vehicle one-driver policy, in their experience this helped to keep down maintenance costs as well as increasing operating efficiency. Pride in the job was certainly in evidence, if the appearance of the fleet was a reliable reflection.

One of the Scammell units was kept in permanent show condition by its conscientious driver.

Many saw this vehicle returning to Harts Lane after a normal day's work and were astonished to see the engine, looking though it was ready for Earls Court, clearly visible through transparent plastics panels in each side of the bonnet. The unconventional bonnet had been modified by the company at the driver's request. Although the company's then familiar emblem depicting a bird carrying a parcel in its beak, with the words 'As the Crow Flies' is purely symbolic, the standing of Crow Carrying was much more than a symbol it was one of Mr. Crow's favourite slogans: 'Progress is the reward of eternal vigilance'.

Photo from Leyland journal

Acoustic shields are provided around the traffic control check-out points

Photo courtesy of Peter J Davies

Scammell Highwayman C138

Photo courtesy of Peter J Davies

Any doubts which might exist as to the use of aluminium for tankers are dispelled by this Scammell articulated outfit which is in regular service after 24 years. During this period there have been three tractor units.

19

Crow Carrying Co Ltd goes to Europe
A One-Man (and vehicle) Common Market 1964

When truck driver Thomas Crawford left home for work in the mornings he always took his suitcase, because he knew it might be weeks before he got home again. For Tom, a 51year old, was the driver of one of Britain's few rigid tankers built specifically for operation on the Continent.

The truck was an eight-wheeled Atkinson, operated by the Crow Carrying Company Ltd, and was the second Atkinson to be used for this type of operation. It carried a variety of pharmaceutical and high-grade chemical products to any country in Western Europe.

Tom pioneered the job nearly four years prior to 1964 when Crow Carrying went into the Continental haulage business. He was treated no differently from any other Crow Carrying driver. Tom was on the AM rates of pay and roughly on the same work. There the similarity ended, because where a British based driver was backed by the organisation of the firm which employed him, Tom also had to be a mobile executive.

His home was the Atkinson de-luxe drivers cab, which had become a mobile spares department, office and occasionally a first-aid post. He carried wads of pink, blue, red and white paper cards, books and folders which got him from country to country, port to port and customs shed to customs shed without undue delay. Fixed to the cab sides and roof were very imaginable kinds of spare part-three complete set of bulbs, extra wiper blades and arms, spare inner tubes, a generator, starter motor, fuel pump and a host of miscellaneous fittings.

Although Tom's foreign language skills would have left room to spare on the back of a postage stamp, Tom found no difficulty in making himself understood. He was his own little Common Marketeer, spreading goodwill wherever he went.

The Atkinson truck was built to confirm to Continental standards. It was fitted with all the extras required by continental countries, riding on eight Dunlop R86 tyres, which carried the vehicle for 25,000 miles in four months. Balanced wheels were used in conjunction with car care safety valves fitted to the rear tyres. The Atkinson lorry Tom drove was a right handed model (which Tom preferred) but was equipped with an intricate series of mirrors which enable him to see down his 'wrong' side with better visibility. "British roads are the best in Europe" said Tom, but he didn't think much of the tourists. The Belgian roads were so bad that his rear mudguards fell off in Liege on one occasion, through the vibration shattering the stays. Whenever he saw a British car pulled up, Tom stopped to ask if he could help, but it would have been hard to find one British family that appreciated his concern.

Tom commented "Continental food is not good says. Breakfast in Paris and dinner in Brussels can play havoc with your stomach, and the water is terrible stuff. I always take the wine, it's much safer, prior 1964 Tom had not taken any holidays on the Continent.

Thomas Crawford at work in Europe on the road

On the left Thomas is unloading

The New Crow Carrying Co Ltd Site At Silvertown 1968

In 1968 The,Crow Carrying Company Ltd moved into a new depot in East London. The site vacated at Barking was to be used for new house building by the local authority. In the meantime, Crow's has developed a 3+ acre site at Silvertown to house its 150 home-based vehicles. The Crow Carrying fleet now had 240 tractive units and 350 tanks.

The company intended to standardise on stainless steel tanks and this in some measure tied up with its move to Silvertown. Most of its customers were in the Silvertown area and before the move each day vehicles were travelling empty for at least six miles on their journeys, while to and from the Barking site. This dead mileage was almost eliminated following the relocation to silvertown

The introduction of stainless steel tanks as standard equipment allowed them to be used for the wide variety of liquids carried by Crow. The tanks, however, would still require cleaning between loads and to ensure that these facilities were readily available the company installed in its new premises a five-point steam bay.

The 35 fitting staff worked around the clock to minimise downtime. From its Manchester depot, Crow operated 25 vehicles on Continental work under TIR. These vehicles carried chemicals and fats to France, Belgium and Sweden, they brought back lard from France and Plasticiser from Sweden. The French and Belgian deliveries were conducted on a door-to-door basis using the company's own drivers, but the Swedish traffic was sent unaccompanied.

Crow Carrying was part of the Transport Development Group (TDG) and its facilities at Silvertown would be used by other group members when their vehicles were in the London area. It was during this time that the company put another six maximum capacity artic outfits into service. The stainless steel 5,500gallon tank-trailers would be pulled by Scammell Handyman Mark 3 tractive units.

Photos courtesy of Terry Edwards

The New Crow's Nest Front Gate and Scammell C48

The New Crow's Nest Building

The New Crow's Nest Yard and Workshop

The New Crow's Nest Yard and Petrol Pumps

As The Crows Fly 1980s

Just 11 years or so prior to 1980, the Crow Carrying Company fleet was entirely British. Scammell Handyman tractors were just replacing the Highwayman model-s that had given great service during the 1960s. From 1980 the tractors used in the company's, exclusively 'tanker operation', were mostly Volvos and DAFs, with a few Seddon 400s being left to wave the Union Jack at the company's headquarters in London's dockland. The dark decade of the 1970s hit the transport industry hard, and Crow Carrying themselves had seen a reduction in their fleet from over 200 trucks to around 100, largely through the loss of a northern subsidiary. As of 1980 they were part of the Transport Development Group, but a retracting market did not explain such a switch in loyalty.

The answer from the engineering Director Jeff Braithwaite sadly had an all too familiar ring to it. At the beginning of the 1970s they ran an exclusively Scammell fleet, but when Scammells were taken over by Leyland they had a lot of problems. The result was that Crow's decided they would never have a one-make fleet again.

Problems surrounded the Leyland-Scammell, the Handyman. Crow Carrying ordered 2 on the basis of their good experience with earlier Watford Built tractors. Maintenance boss Dave Bennett said, they were very poor, the basic reason being that many of the new Leyland parts were just not compatible with the Scammell designs. They reached a point where more units were in the yard than were on the road.

Crow Carrying then took on 7 other makes of lorry and then based their Fleet on the three they had found to give the best combination of reliability and backup, although a few early British Atkinson Borderer, Guys and old ERFs arc worked out their time in Silvertown, under the shadow of the Victoria and Albert dock cranes. The swing towards Volvo came with a test on an early F86. A number were purchased of which 12 examples remained (in 1980). The F7 replacement for the F86 had proved popular for a number of reasons and they made up the biggest single model total at 20.

Six F88 took care of the heavier work. Of the DAFs, nine were 2800s four 2300s and the remaining 2200s. The Seddons were mostly 400 series tractors, although a couple of M rigid tankers were used for small loads. Although Crows settled on their choice of makes, they would still take other vehicles on appraisal if they looked good on paper. They had a DKSE DAF on trial which soon joined the ranks permanently. Jeff Braithwaite said, "we put service back-up very high on our list of priorities when looking at new models". They priviously tried a MAN tractor some time ago, which was a good truck but they decided not to take it because the back-up was not as good as with the DAFs and Volvos. "I am an Englishman but I must say that we have found these vehicles are better than any of the British makes". said Dave

The swing to imports had not been totally smooth though. The F86 gave a lot of trouble in the early days, thanks to the TD70C engines, tendency to blow head gaskets with monotonous regularity. The pistons also needed replacing in most of the trucks before their third birthday. The problems were a blot on their copybook, but as Dave Bennett explained, they cured it by bringing out the TD70E engine in the F7, Dave felt it too early to tell about long life reliability, but said "so far they have been really good". The only exceptions being a couple of problems with turbo impellers. On one unit the wheel developed excessive play, while in the other the fan was found to have some blade damage, though the missing bits do not seem to have caused any other injury to the engines

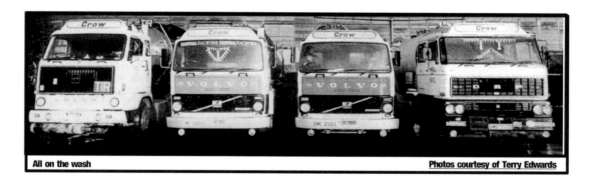

All on the wash   Photos courtesy of Terry Edwards

As The Crows Fly 1980s

With the DAFs things were good too, although a differential pinion bearing broke on one fairly aged example. A gearbox problem on a DKTD 28(1) model still under warranty allowed Harris, the local DAF dealer at Purfleet, to provide just the sort of back-up that Crows put such a premium on. Jeff Braithwaite said we had a gearbox failure on this truck in the early to middle afternoon, phoned Harris' and they said that there wasn't another gearbox like it in the country. The next morning, they had one in their depot at 8.30a.m., which had been brought from Holland
with the carry sleeper-cabin'.

DAF drivers complained that they were too cold at night. The matter was the subject of negotiation between Crows and the Unions at the depot and couldn't just be solved by putting a cab heater in. The problem was that most of Crow`s tractors were 'pet-regged' fitted with heat shields and nylon covered wiring in accordance with regulations for carrying inflammable substances. Crow thought a cab heater might be outlawed by the CYCM stricter ADR regulations necessary for carrying volatile loads across the Channel and to which most of their vehicles complied. They intended to fit a heater for an ADR inspection to test the ban theory.

Dave Bennett believed the back-up on the Seddons was inferior to the imports, despite the fact that there were three dealers within easy reach. Premature wear on clutches had been a major bugbear, and rear hub oil seals had to be replaced on the 4005 with regularity. The factory option underslung frontal exhausts demanded by the 'pet-regs' dropped off rather too often for Dave's liking.

Seddon Atkinson C64 on the tank wash   **Photos courtesy of Terry Edwards**

As The Crows Fly 1980s

Despite identifying these complaints., Dave Bennett was happy with all three chosen makes, pointing out that they were the survivors from a wide range of trucks that Crow had sampled.

The seriousness with which Crow were dealing with the 'cold cab' complaint was indicative of the importance they attached to driver acceptance of any vehicle they bought. And again unhappy for Seddon, the Atkinson comes out third best in this area too. Dave Bennett said: 'The F7 cab is superb, really comfortable, and the drivers really like them. The DAFs are liked too and against them, the Seddon are not as good, in our experience'.

Crow fitted sleeper cabs as a matter of policy, primarily because the drivers preferred to stay with the truck while away, which was often the case with the Contract and Hire work that took Crow vehicles all over Britain and Europe. As well as 'pet-reg' modifications, Crow trucks had special bolt-on fuel tanks mounted behind the cab in the form of a cross-chassis catwalk.

The same practical thinking had been worked into the pumps fitted to most of the tractors. Instead of direct mechanical drive, the PTO drives a hydraulic system which can be connected to a compressor or a pump for discharging tanks. The hydraulic power is switched to either unit by pipes with self-sealing Suzi type connectors, making the operation quick and clean. The machinery was mounted on a steel section frame that could be unbolted and removed complete in a matter of minutes. The Seddons actually had two PTO's, but the Crow-designed system was used on them as well. Dave Bennett said that the chief advantage of hydraulic, as opposed to mechanical P.T.O drive, is the gradual power take-up. The only other method was the fitting of anti-roll bars on the DAF front axles to eliminate the problems of tanker contents movement being carried through into the tractor.

Since Its foundation by Mr Latimer Crow in 1920, the Crow Carrying Company had concentrated on tanker work, restricting themselves to liquids. Even so the range of loads was vast, and their treatment presented a wider range of problems than in any other part of the haulage industry. The need to make every load pay had led them to abandon their policy of each trip being made on a return basis. They then had to get a return load in order to make money in the majority of cases. Obviously this presented major difficulties when the loads there and back could be as different as drinking water and vinegar, so Crow's negotiated a network of specialist cleaning contacts up and down the country.

They had 145 trailers, from Crane Fruehauf and Universal Bulk Handling, with a few Scammells.

Those were divided into groups, some for general work, some for heavy oil and other hazardous loads, and some specialist units for commodities that required delicate handling. The 'casual hire' tankers were insulated stainless steel, mounted like all their trailers on Norde rubber suspension. Dave Bennett said; It is lighter and quieter than leaf springing and maintenance is nil while the trailer is running. Also the £240 price of a set of four rubbers, and the two-day job of fitting them every three years was preferable to the easier, but more frequent attention leaf springs demanded.

Chocolate is one of the most difficult loads to transport and illustrates the problems some tanker operations create. The chocolate should be kept between 120degF and 140degF, too cold and it cannot be pumped, too hot and it goes white or burns. These strict limits forced Crow's to have trailers specially built for the job of delivering the gooey stuff to cake and biscuit manufacturers. Other substances like lard could be heated by pumping steam through radiating pipes inside the tank and then discharged.

Jeff Braithwate Manager

Silvertown workshop   Photos courtesy of Terry Edwards

As The Crows Fly 1980s

Heating the chocolate through radiating pipes was not acceptable as the chocolate next to the pipes just burnst.

The chocolate tankers built by UBH, worked on the vacuum Hask principal. They have a central chamber for the load, surrounded by two thin outer chambers. The middle one of the three is heated with water to the required temperature, then the water is drawn off to leave a vacuum.

Hazardous loads ranged from concentrated Sulphuric acid to heavy fuel oil, to Phenol, and Crow had a special steam-cleaning bay equipped to dispose of the nastiest kinds of chemical residue. A settling tank was used to remove the worst of the waste before the washing water was allowed into the sewers, and the remainder was collected and dumped on a poison waste site in Essex every few weeks.

Crow were fastidious about cleaning the stainless steel tanks, which were tackled with steam power, using various types of detergent. The mixture would be sprayed around with a spinning nozzle dropped in through the top hatch. Dave Bennett dealt with the maintenance, in four bays, two long enough for trailers as well. All Crow trucks were hand painted, as they said it lasted much longer. Engineering director Jeff Braithwaite ran the fleet of Volvos DAFs and Seddons though a few old models like Guy still survived. Vacuum petrol tanks gave 50gallon extra range, useful when carrying precarious loads like chocolate in vacuum principal tanker. Acid-proof suits were part of rescue gear safety and were part of the Emergency Load Transfer Scheme set up by the RHA. Their only box van sat in the corner of a Compound where the hazardous load tankers were kept during overnight stops. Inside this van was also a collection of tools, pumps, pipes, fittings, absorbent granules, breathing apparatus and acid-proof suits, ready for use if there was a need to transfer a liquid load in an emergency. People in the company were on call 24 hours a day, but as Braithwaite said there is the best part of three grand sitting down at the end of our yard, but I sincerely hope we will never need to use it. If they ever do, at least they will have the experience to cope, experience earned the hard way making a living.

Photos courtesy of Terry Edwards

Crow Carrying Co Ltd
Vans through the Years

Workshop Van 1970s   **Photo courtesy of pm photography**

Photo courtesy of Terry Edwards

WorkshopStores
Tralier Original above & Artist Impression Below

Workshop Transit Van 1980s   **Photo courtesy of Terry Edwards**

MAGNIFICENT SEVEN

At Crow Carrying Company, in the late 1960s
there were 7 drivers who called themselves the 'Magnificent Seven', started by Yorkie and Bubbles who, when on a contract delivering Nitric acid from Grimsby, decided they wanted to run the contract how they thought it should be run. The contract ran from between 7 to 9 months, and what eventually stemmed from this was the 'Royals', which more drivers decided they wanted to join.
Here are some photographs of the original 'Magnificent Seven'. **Photos courtesy of Terry Edwards**

Crow Carrying Co Ltd Drivers Profile Bill E. Wheeler 1926 - 1960

Billie started driving for Crow Carrying in 1926. His first lorry was a AEC C26, pictured below, which he drove for 15 years. He also kept the AEC manufactures plate – 1918, also pictured below. The next lorry was an International bonneted C33.

Billie had was a Bedford C150. He never drove Artics he said he was just happy with rigid. Billie is also seen below collecting his 20 year safety medal.

In later days when Billie carried tar, it was noted among drivers, that he wore the same coat for all the tar contracts, without washing it. It must have been as stiff as a board. Billie got his 25year safety medal and drove for Crow Carrying for 34 years.

Photos Courtesy of Bill E Wheeler

25 Year Safty Medal

AEC C.26 Name Plate

Bill at Crow Carrying awards night

Photos from the 40th anniversary of Crow Carrying Co booklet

Over 20 years service medals

INTERNATIONAL C33

Bedford C33

Bedford C33

Crow Carrying Co Ltd Drivers Profile Jack Threshie 1930-1980

Jack joined Crow Carrying straight from school as a drivers' mate, at a time when solid tyres were used and chain driven lorries. Jack eventually went on to drive them.

Jack drove a C19 Scammell and an Atkinson 8 wheeler C181, which he took to Europe on a regular basis. Jack also drove a C7 Scammell Highwayman, in which he won Driver of the Year. He was on contracts for Lesmys Chocolate driving a Scammell, and he finished up on the Marley Tiles contract in 1979. Jack retired from Crows in 1980 and was the only driver to put in 50 years service. For his 50 years service, the Management presented him a wall clock. After his retirement he started gardening, he said the work kept him alive. He was right because he died at the ripe old age of 94.

From 1930 to 1980 Jack definitely saw the transport industry change. He was certainly one of a kind, and he thought Crow's was a good firm to work. I wonder what he would have thought about the transport industry to-day?

Atkinson 8 wheeler C.181 driven by Jack Threshie goes to Europe **Photo courtesy of Jack Threshie**

Jack Threshie won driver of the year in a Scammell Highwayman C.7
Photo courtesy of Jack Threshie

Crow Carrying Co Ltd Drivers Profile James Matthews
1940-1968

Before James joined Crow Carrying he worked for a company called Fisher Renwick. At Crow's the lorry James drove was a Scammell Highwayman, in which he carried a number of liquids, including Linseed oil, Vinegar, Paraffin, Aircraft fuel, Seawater, Apple juice and finally Chocolate. The last photograph below shows   his AEC Mercury fleet 160.

James drove long distance all across England and Scotland. James started driving when he was 15 years old, he drove Scammells and Tankers for 31 years. James was away working for 5 days out of 7. He also drove solo and always managed to finish the job despite very bad weather. James never had an accident.

Top two photos courtesy of James Matthews

James Matthews & Grandaughter & Scammell C223

James Matthews and hes AEC C160 UMX 108F 1967

James Matthews Scammell Highwayman reg 6792EV fleet 106 **Photo courtesy of pm photography**

Crow Carrying Co Ltd Drivers Profile Charlie Hawksbee
1948-1965

Charlie first joined Crow Carrying in 1948 leaving in 1951, he rejoined the company again in 1963. How did you get a driving job with Crows Charlie? I saw a tanker go past the other way while I was on the bus. It had the sign on the back 'AS THE CROW FLIES', so I decided to write and apply for a job.

Charlie remembered some of his old pals at Crows - Harry Fowler, Ernie Gibbons, Georgie Foster, Bill Golding and Davy Doe and from the fitter's shop Van Deens and Johnny Hairs. Charlie drove the Bedford fleet 28 and his favourite was the International Fleet 30.

Charlie never got to drive the Scammells at Crows during 1948 to 1951 because he never had the experience. He left Crows to go to Canada only to come back in 1963. When he came back he told the office he now had experience in the Scammell shed, so he was allowed to drive the Scammells, but he didn't really have the experience.

Charlie enjoyed general work the best. He left Crows for the final time in 1965.

The other companies who Charlie worked for as a tanker driver included Pointers of Norwich and Silwoods plus twice for Bill Golding. He also worked for a Private Eye and as a chauffeur driver

Charlie said he never went abroad he just loved general work and they were good old times

Charlie recalls his Bedford C28 also simler to these one C49

Charlie recalls the Dennis at Crows C73 JXB 342 Reconstruction photo

Crow Carrying Co Ltd Drivers Profile George Liddard Snr
1948-1963
Alfred Liddard 1960-1985 & George Liddard Jnr 1963-1970s

George Snr joined Crow Carrying in 1948, in 1960 his son Alf also joined the company as a driver. The lorry Alf drove was the famous C127 Scammell Highwayman. Alf painted over the famous see through bonnet. He also had various other lorries like the C47 DAF 2800. Alf finished at Crows in 1985.

George Jnr joined Crow Carrying in 1963 also as a driver. Before driving for Crows, George Jnr worked for Kingsford Haulage, thereafter he applied to work at Crow Carrying Company.

George Jnr was the last of his family to work for Crows. The lorries George Jnr drove were a Scammell Highwayman C113, on a Benzene contract, and a 4 wheeler Bedford on the Shell contract. George Jnr also drove a Scania C96 on other contracts delivering Esso, Chevron and Caxton Chocolate.

George Liddad senior drove a Scammell simlar to this one 1948   **Photo courtesy of Nick Baldwin**

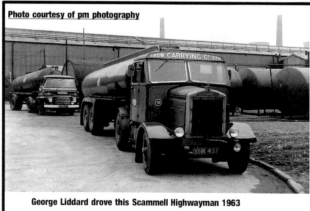

Photo courtesy of pm photography

George Liddard drove this Scammell Highwayman 1963

Alfred Liddad junior drove this DAF 2800 1980s

Photos courtesy of Terry Edwards

Crow Carrying Co Ltd Drivers Profile John Smith 1951-1978

Before joining Crow Carrying, John worked for a company called C.W. Rudd. When he joined Crows his father, Bert Smith also worked there. John drove many lorries during his time at Crows. He remembers the C70 Scammell Highwayman Registration LTW419, the C44 Scammell Highwayman Registration LVX41, the C10 Scammell Highwayman Registration VHK438, the C79 Scammell Highwayman Registration NPU718 the C111 Scammell Highwayman Registration UEV996 the C55 Scammell Highwayman Registration 1523F, the C173 Scammell Highwayman Registration 4095HK, the C173 was made into a Corgi model. The C35 Scammell Highwayman Registration YTW973, the C120 Scammell Highwayman Registration 87XNO, the C241 Scammell Handyman Registration XBY857G, and the C133 Foden Registration GMM352N.
John went on contacted to Chevron while working at Crows but left to join Chevron itself in 1978.
He was made redundant from Chevron in 1984. John and his father Bert Smith were the only father and son to get 25 year gold watches working for Crows.

John and his Scammell Highwayman C79

John Smiths father Bert Smith and his Scammell Highwayman C25

All but one Photo courtesy of John Smith

Heres John washing inside his tank on C55 John Smith & C55

Scammell C120 on contract to Chevron

Photo courtesy of Terry Edwards

Crow Carrying Co Ltd Drivers Profile George Paramore 1954-1968

George joined Crow Carrying in 1954 finishing in 1968. George had previously worked for British Paints. When he was made redundant from British Paints, George went to the pub with his dad and met up with Jimmy Mathews, an old friend of his dad's. Jimmy Mathews worked at Crows. George told Jimmy that he had just been made redundant and that he had no other work to go to, but Jimmy said, no problem. When On the Monday morning George met up with Jimmy again he said, you have an interview at Crows for Monday morning 9:00 am sharp, just go and see Mr. Reynolds.

So George went along to see Mr. Reynolds. When George arrived at Crow's yard, Mr. Reynolds asked him what are you doing here? George said, I'm here for an interview, Mr. Reynolds asked who had sent him, looking a bit bewildered George said Jimmy Mathews, well that's ok then. The reason being Mr. Reynolds and Jimmy Matthews were both freemasons. Jimmy did that sort of thing most of the time, without telling Reynolds. So George got the job. George drove for 18 months then went into the workshop in the electrical department. George only drove on seasonal work, in an S type Bedford C137, but when that work dried up he would go into the workshop and help out on the electrical side. He would also go out with Alfie Martin from the workshop in the ex military AEC 7.7 breakdown lorry, to other breakdowns. It had a 4 ton direct pull winch. George was needed more and more in the workshop and eventually ended up staying there.

The workshop at Barking had full length pits for the trailers and ramps for the Scammells. George explained why the tanks were number marked for the different liquids they carried; from peas to wine, acid, milk and chocolate.

George finished at Crow Carrying when the firm moved from Barking to Silvertown, it was a long commute for him. He told me he was so happy to recall the memories about the old days.

Georges mates Jack Brice,Bill Baily

Georges mate Van Veen

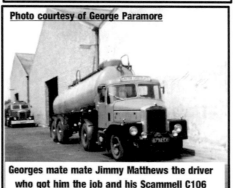
Georges mate mate Jimmy Matthews the driver who got him the job and his Scammell C106

Artist Impression photo of a A.E.C breakdown wagon which George drove for the workshop

Crow Carrying Co Ltd Drivers Profile Henry Reilly 1954-1985

Before joining Crow Carrying Henry worked for a demolition company. At Crows he drove 7 examples of the Scammell Highwayman. There was one regular Scammell Highwayman from 1963 with a Gardener engine, Registration 367 SOO, which was on contract to Loders Nucoline.

As a senior driver, he nearly always got the first new lorry that came along. Crow's became dissatisfied with the Scammell Handyman so bought a Scania, Registration FLK 288J after that Henry got a Seddon Atkinson NMC 395R which he felt wasn't as good. His favourite lorry was a DAF 2800 Registration VMK 329S, it was a good all-rounder and he liked it more than his previous lorry which was a Volvo F7 Registration HMU 256W. Henry saw the early days at Barking and the move to Silvertown, good friends with Jimmy Matthews and Dicky Bird, he remembers delivering water to concerts, one of which was the Rolling Stones at Knebworth. He also drove abroad to Holland and Italy.

Henry enjoyed working at Crows. He said, them good days won't come back again.

Photo courtesy of Henry Reilly

1963 with a Gardener engine, reg 367 SOO which was on contract to Loder Nucoline.

Photo courtesy of Terry Edwards

Scania reg FLK 288J C77 1970

Photo courtesy of Terry Edwards

Seddon Atkinson NMC 395R which was't a good lorry C22 1976

Crow Carrying Co Ltd Drivers Profile Larry Lythall 1956-1985

Larry was known as 'Bubbles'. Larry was given this nickname because when he had a few drinks he blew bubbles from his nose. Larry joined Crow Carrying in 1956.
Larry drove various lorries like the Scammell Handyman C221 and Volvo F6 C72. Larry Lythall and Rob York started the 'Magnificent Seven', which they formed together whilst working on a contract for Nitric acid in Grimsby. During this contract, they worked away from home for 7 to 9 months of the year. Larry also drove in Europe. Larry finished at Crows in 1985.

Photos courtesy of Terry Edwards

Photos courtesy of Terry Edwards

Bubbles & Scammell C224 above 1968

This is Bubbles last lorry Volvo F7 C75   1979

Crow Carrying Co Ltd Drivers Profile George Robinson
1957-1970s

George joined Crow Carrying in the late 1950s, he drove a Scammell Highwayman C130, as pictured below, he did general tanking work.
George also drove a Scammell Highwayman II C164 on contract to DCL also pictured below
He then went on Gulf Oil and Texaco contracts.

The two photos below are courtesy of George Robinson

George Robinson Driver and work mates fitters names unknown with Scammell Highwayman C130

Scammell Highwayman C164 on D.C.L Contract   Photos courtesy of George Robinson

Crow Carrying Co Ltd Drivers Profile Jackie Barnfield
1950s -1985

Jackie was one of the biggest characters at Crows. Jackie drove quite a few lorries. He drove a Scammell Highwayman Registration WVW 755. fleet 117 on contract for ABRAC. He also did general work and as far as I know he never went abroad. Jackie also drove a DAF 2500 registration WML 405T and a DAF 2800 registration WML 30T fleet 49.
Jackie was made redundant in1985, and said he loved his time at Crows.

Jackie and his DAF 2500 Fleet 55 1978   Photo courtesy of Terry Edwards

Jackie and his DAF 2800 Fleet 49 1978   Photo courtesy of Terry Edwards

Crow Carrying Co Ltd Drivers Profile Tony King 1957-1963

Tony joined Crow Carrying at a time when you had to be sponsored by someone who already worked for the company, and Jimmy Priest was that sponsor (he was a driver there).
Tony delivered Tar and Creosote in a 4 wheeler Bedford C16. He then went on various other contracts for Crow's, Shell at Fulham driving a Bedford C160 then DCL driving an S type Bedford C75 and a Maldsley C74 delivering to British Vinegars. He was also on Shell Lube Oil every winter.
Tony left Crows in 1963 and moved away getting a job with Upton Oil Company where he worked for 20 years.

Tony King &
Bedford C16
Photos courtesy of Tony King

Bedford C160   Photo courtesy of pm photography

Crow Carrying Co Ltd Drivers Profile Ray Oliff 1958 -1961

Ray Oliff joined Crow Carrying in 1958 finishing up in 1961. Before joining Crows Ray worked for a company called Yiddel Davis or Davis Brothers.

When Ray first drove for Crows, he drove a small 4 wheeler, then moving up to an Arctic, like the 10 ton Bedford fleet 152, contracted to Pinch & Johnson's. He wasn't allowed on Scammells because he had a clubbed foot, which made him all the more determined to be the best tanker driver that he could be. They once asked him to go on the disabled register and he said no.

The drivers he got on well with were George Walker and Danny Piper and from the workshop, Lenny Mulley. The contracts he worked on were P.R Chemicals and Pinching Johnson's and May & Bakers. Ray used to have nights out in digs and once or twice slept in his cab, which was called a 'nutdown' cab because it was only designed for short rest periods, but he used it once for night work. He also drove a Morris, BMC fleet 101 and a Bedford petrol engine fleet which was also C101, and a Leyland Comet unknown fleet. Ray never drove abroad he stayed in the UK. His favourite cafe was Mays cafe in Barking near Crow's office and depot.

The contract he liked working the on most was delivering to Preston Docks in Preston for May & Bakers in the Morris C101.

Ray's comments on working for Crows was that they had the best paint work and Thomas Allen had the best maintenance.

. Ray left Crows after they wouldn't pay for a phone call when he was working up the road.

Ray went on to drive Scammells for Thomas Allen from 1961 to 1966. Ray then went to United Molasses and retired in 1988.

Ray drove for over 40years, his comments were, they were the good old days.

Photo courtesy of Ray Oliff

Ray Oliff with his Bedford C152 at home

and wife   Photo courtesy of Ray Oliff

To the right
Ray' Morris C101
in Manchester Depot

Courtesy of pm photography

Crow Carrying Co Ltd Drivers Profile Brian Smith 1959 - 1979

Before Brian joined Crow Carrying, he drove for Levon Coal Merchants. Brian got the job at Crow Carrying after seeing a Crow's lorry being driven down Harts Road. When he first started he was told he would have to take a road test in a BMC Arctic. He said he was a bit nervous, but was ok because he had driven a BMC before. Brian didn't go on general tanking he went on contract to Loders & Nucoline Ltd.

The lorries Brian drove were a 4 wheeler AEC Mercury, Scammell Highwayman, Volvo F86 and a DAF 2300, which he felt was very under powered.

Now Brian liked a bet,and he regularly 'bet for his breakfast'. He would say to his workmates, I bet you I can lift that butler sink up over my head, the sink was really heavy.and Just to check on the weight his workmates would first have a go at it, even guys much bigger then Brian, but they could never lift it, He would then pick it up and lift it straight above his head and win himself a breakfast, it worked every time. Unknown to his workmates he would practice lifting that butler sink every day.

The pictures below are similar to the lorries that Brian drove.

Photo courtesy of pm photography

Photo courtesy of pm photography

Crow Carrying Co Ltd Drivers Profile Phillp Hartwell 1950s -1985

Phil joined Crow Carrying in the 1950s. His nickname was 'Phil the Flute'. Phil drove general work with some contracts work and abroad work. Phil had a TK Bedford C147 in which he entered the driver of the year competition. Phil also had an Atkinson C79, Volvo C165, Scammell Handyman C19 and a DAF C94. Phil left Crows in 1972 with a group of drivers to start up a new firm but it did not go well so Phil found himself back with Crows in 1973. Phil finished in 1985 and then joined Wincanton eventually retiring in 1996.

Photo Courtesy of NA3T Archive

Phil at the driver of the year with his TK BEDFORD C147

Photo courtesy of Terry Edwards

Phil in depot along side C19 Scammell Handyman

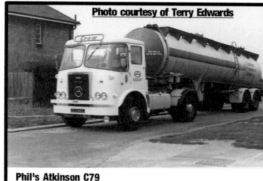
Photo courtesy of Terry Edwards

Phil's Atkinson C79

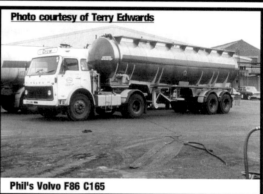
Photo courtesy of Terry Edwards

Phil's Volvo F86 C165

Photo courtesy of Terry Edwards

Phil in cab of Volvo F86 C165

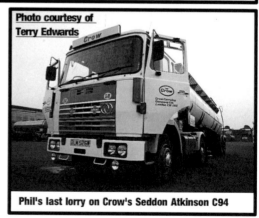
Photo courtesy of Terry Edwards

Phil's last lorry on Crow's Seddon Atkinson C94

Crow Carrying Co Ltd Drivers Profile Gus Gascoin 1960 -1980

Before Gus joined Crow Carrying he worked for the navy. Prior to this he drove for the Co-Operative. In 1960 Gus decided to cycle over to Crow's Barking depot, to see if any jobs were available. When he approached security at the gate, the guard told him he would stand a better chance of getting a job if he wore a tie, so he cycled back home. When he went back to Crows he got the job.

Gus stayed at Crows for 20 years until 1980. He drove various lorries three of which are pictured below. The first was C139 a Scammell Highwayman, which had just been cleaned at the Barking depot. Drivers always washed their own lorries. The second photo is a Guy Big J C193, which is shown at the Silvertown depot having a wash. The third photo is of an Atkinson Borderer which was on contract to BP at Shell Haven depot in 1972. Being on contract had a significant effect on Gus, he said I never had a new lorry, but I loved the ones I drove.

After leaving Crows, Gus spent 5 years with Redbridge Borough Council driving for the Parks Department. He still meets up with old colleagues from Crows like Charlie Hawksbee.

Photo Courtesy of Gus Gascloin
Gus's Scammell C139

Gus's C193 Guy   Photo Courtesy of Gus Gascloin

Photo Courtesy of Gus Gascloin

Gus's Atkinson C85

Crow Carrying Co Ltd Drivers Profile Johnny Cargill
1960s -1980s

Johnny joined Crow Carrying in the 1960s. Johnny was a much liked driver, he was also one of the 'Magnificent Seven'. Johnny was on general work and contract work such as Sarson's Vinegar. Johnny drove an AEC Mandator C167, Scammell Handyman C19, and a DAF 2300. He left Crows in the 1980s and started working as a bus driver.

Johnny Caygill & A.E.C C167 1967

Johnny Caygill in cab DAF 2300 C90

Johnny Caygill & DAF 2300 loading C90 1980

Johnny Caygill & Scammell Handyman C19 1968

Crow Carrying Co Ltd Drivers Profile Alf Tucker Snr
1926 -1966
& Alf Tucker Jnr 1961 - 1966

Alf Snr joined Crow Carrying in 1926 finishing in 1966. When Alf joined the company he drove chain driven Scammells - C12 and C40. The various contracts Alf worked on included Shell Oil and various others. Alf's favourite Café was Mays. Alf finished at Crows when he had a heart attack.

Alf Jnr joined his father at Crow Carrying in 1961. The job he had before Crows was driving for Sharps on high sided tippers. The trucks Alf Jnr drove were a Maldsley an Albion a Scammell and an International. The contracts Alf Jnr worked on were - Segas Wines, British Vinegar's, Carless Cable & Leonard, British Motor Corp', Pain Poppets Chocolate, May & Bakers, McCleans, Sunlight Soap, and L & N. Alf Jnr's favourite Café was also Mays in Barking.

Alf Jnr got on with many of the drivers at Crows, but the one that stood out the most was Milky Sams. Alf said he also remembered Mr. Langley and Van Veen in the workshop. After Alf left Crows he had various other driving jobs whilst also working for himself. The other companies he worked for were Texaco and Wincanton. He said the time he had at Crows was a good one. In remembering those days, he told how Herbert Crow used to buy thick warm driving coats for the drivers and one day Herbert was walking through the Scammell shed when he saw a driver laying under a Scammell, on top of one of those thick warm coats in a pool of oil. That was last time Herbert Crow bought drivers any coats again.

Herbert Crow paid cash for the new Scammells and it was Alf's job at the time to take the cash or cheque and pick them up and drive them back to the yard.

Alf's dad Alf Tuckers Scammell C12 parked at home

Photo courtesy of Alf Tucker

Crow Carrying Co Ltd Drivers Profile Jack Browning 1962 - 1985

Before joining Crow Carrying, Jack was in the Merchant Navy working on tankers. Prior to that he worked for a transport firm, name unknown.

Jack started working at Crow Carrying in 1962 and finished in 1985. He got a job with Crows when working for another transport company, his lorry got a puncture near the Crow's depot. He walked to Crow's yard for help, but soon got more than he bargained for, they offered him a job and he took it, he never looked back. The trucks Jack drove were various 4 wheeler motors and an Atkinson 8 wheeler fleet 181, which he drove throughout Europe. Jack had various other motors, a Scania and then a Volvo F88, which was his favourite, then a Renault fleet 112. Jack wasn't on contract work just abroad work. Jack liked going to the South of France, Finland and Denmark. Jack's first trip to Europe was to Switzerland. He got on with most of the drivers at Crows, although his best mate there was Rob York (Yorkie).

After being made redundant in 1985, Jack took a job with Tankfreight, eventually retiring in the 1990s. Jack said Crow's was a firm where if you fitted in, that was great, but if you didn't you might as well go to work for Thomas Allen Ltd. Jack was one of the 'Royals' who had their run of Europe and they took their own time and ran the job how they wanted, which suited them down to the ground. That was just the way it was back then.

Jack's nickname was 'handsome Jack', named by his dad's co-workers. Jack also mentioned that at the Barking depot, Herbert H Crow had put a time capsule of Crow memorabilia in the roof of the Scammell shed for old time sake, it maybe myth or true, who knows?

Photo courtesy of Terry Edwards

Jack Browning had the first Scania in the 70s fleet 35 1970

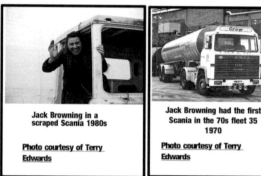

Jack Browning in a scraped Scania 1980s

Photo courtesy of Terry Edwards

Jack Browning had the first Scania in the 70s fleet 35 1970

Photo courtesy of Terry Edwards

Photo courtesy of Terry Edwards

Jack Browning this Renault in the 80s fleet 112 1983

Crow Carrying Co Ltd Drivers Profile Tom Lord 1963 -1985

Tom Lord started Crow Carrying Co in 1963 at the Manchester depot He went on general tanker work and went on many contracts which included I.C.I and British Malt Vinegar.Tom also went to
Europe which included a journey from Manchester to Italy other trips included Germany Holland Belgium France and many more and all over the UK.Tom drove many different lorries like a AEC Mandator C161 and a Volvo F88 C64. He also had duties of picking up and dropping off
units to different depots.In 1984 Tom and the other driver at to move to Widnes depot and in 1985 Crow

Carrying Co was finished and Tom at to move on
Tom said he had some great friends AT Crows and some great times on the road at work

Photo courtesy of Tom Lord

Tom Lord and his AEC Mantator C161

Photo courtesy of Tom Lord

Tom Lords Volvo C64 also with friends and family

47

Crow Carrying Co Ltd Drivers Profile Alexander Wilkins
1963 - 1985

Alexander Wilkins joined Crow Carrying in 1963. Alexander was known as 'Joe the Crow'. Joe drove for Crows for 22 years. Joe was one of the' Magnificent Seven' and one of the 'Royals'.
The contracts that Joe worked on were various. Being a 'Royal' he was on general work and worked abroad.
The lorries Joe drove were a Scammell Highwayman, Scammell Handyman, and AEC Mandator fleets, registration unknown. Joe also drove a DAF 2800 C110 and a Volvo F7 C84.
Joe was made redundant in 1985 and finished up at Wincantons Tankers. Joe was also known as Mr. Crow. He was one of the top earners at Crows at the time.

VOLVO C80 simler to what Alex drove   **Photo courtesy of Terry Edwards**

Alex and his DAF 2800 C110   **Photo courtesy of Terry Edwards**

Crow Carrying Co Ltd Drivers Profile Bill Golding Snr 1940s & Bill Golding Jnr 1964 -1973

Bill Jnr joined Crow Carrying in 1964. He was mostly on contract work to Sternol Cable Compounds, delivering Lube Oil all over the home counties starting out from Millwall. Bill Jnr drove a Bedford J type 4 wheeler fleet 227. He followed his father who started his own Company called Golding.
Bill Snr started working for Crow Carrying in 1948 until 1972. Bill was on contract to the Caxton Chocolate fleet, 106 Reg 7692EV. Bill Snr also drove a Scammell Highwayman fleet 96 PTW 773. and when he finished at Crows he started his own tanker firm Goldings then joined by son Bill Golding Jnr

This is simlar to Bill Goldings Bedford one fleet number off his 228. 1965
Photo courtesy of pm photography

Photo courtesy of Bill Golding

Bill Goldings fathers Scammell C95

49

Crow Carrying Co Ltd Drivers Profile Robert York 1964 - 1985

Prior to working for Crow Carrying Company Robert York, nicknamed 'Yorkie' worked for London Transport as a bus driver. In the early 1960s he was driving for the Richmond Sausage Company. Whilst working for Richmond's, he drove a Bedford. He joined Crow Carrying in 1964. It was at Crows that he got into his first tanker. He drove various 4 wheelers - AEC and Albion, but his first permanent lorry was a Scammell Highwayman fleet 112. He also drove a Leyland Beaver fleet 115 then a AEC Mandator with a 13 Lt engine, which was very fast, fleet 27. Then he drove a Scammell Handyman fleet 141, a Scania 110 fleet 102, which he said was the best for comfort.

His next lorry was a DAF 2800 fleet 44, followed by another DAF 2800 fleet 104, this was his last lorry working for Crows before the company changed to Buckley Tankers in 1984.

Rob then joined LPG Transport, where he was contracted to BP Chemicals. He had a Seddon Atkinson fleet number unknown. In 1985 he joined Calor Transport for a while, and drove a 'b' series ERF fleet unknown.

In 1986 he joined Tankfreight on the Exxon Chemicals contract, where he drove an Iveco.

In 1991 Rob ended his driving days working for Tankfreight. During that time, he helped me get my HGV Licence and a job with Tankfreight. As the saying goes, it's not what you know, it's who you know. Thanks to Rob, my father, I had 40 years of driving knowledge passed to me, which helped me on my way to earning a good living.

DAF fleet 104 and Yorkie 1982   Photos courtesy of Terry Edwards

Crow Carrying Co Ltd Drivers Profile Roger Walsh 1964 - 1985

Before joining Crow Carrying, Roger worked for Keens Tipper Company. Roger had tried previously to get a job with Crows and was only successful on his second attempt. Roger drove a TK Bedford, Volvo F86, a Mercedes and a DAF 2800.
He drove on British Vinegar, contracts he did general work and abroad work. Roger was one of the 'Royals', who were able to pick and choose what work they did.
Roger had the nickname 'Roger the Dodger', by name and by nature, no explanation needed.
After leaving Crows Roger joined Silver Roadways then Calor Transport, LPG then TDG which was once part of Crows. So you could say he went back home

Roger in the Shetlands DAF 2800 C43

Roger just got off the boat at Dover DAF 2800 C102

Photo courtesy of pm photography

Roger unloading with his Mercedes C107

Photo courtesy of Roger Walsh

e.

Crow Carrying Co Ltd Drivers Profile Bill Humphreys 1965-1975

Before Bill joined Crow Carrying he worked for the Lyons Company. His best mate, Robert York 'Yorkie' got him the job with Crows. The contracts Bill worked on were British Vinegar, Shell Petrol Roundtree, Caxton Chocolate, Johnson & Johnson and the Pure Lard Company. Apart from contract work Bill was on general work and abroad work.

The lorries Bill drove were a Scammell Highwayman 3, registration OWC 94 unknown fleet number, a Scammell Handyman and an AEC Mandator fleets and registration also unknown.

Bill Left Crows when he was next in line for a new vehicle, but they decided to give it to another driver, Jack Browning 'Handsome Jack', this made Bill a bit despondent. Bill left Crows and got a job at the Post Office.

Heres Bill & his Scammell
Photo courtesy of Bill Humphrey

Heres Bill & his mate Johnny Caygill in a Publicity photo 1968   Photo courtesy of Terry Edwards

Crow Carrying Co Ltd Drivers Profile Terry Edwards 1965-1985

Terry joined Crow Carrying in 1965, he also became Crow's official photographer. He loved working for Crows, you can see this in his photographs.
Terry drove various lorries in the 1960s. In the 1970s he had a Volvo F86 C165 and a Volvo F7. Then he became the yard foreman.
When Crow Carrying finished in 1985, Terry was given the job of dealing with the stock clean up, making sure the lorries went where they were supposed to go and the office and workshop clearance.
When Terry left he got a job as a bus driver.

Below are some of Terry's great photo's

Terry at the docks with C165

Terry with C165   Photos courtesy of Terry Edwards

Terry at the truck wash with C165 above & below

Terry's promo picture

More Terry Edwards's Photo's

Photos courtesy of Terry Edwards

54

Crow Carrying Co Ltd Drivers Profile Joe Curtis 1965 - 1985

Joe joined Crow Carrying in 1965. He was on general and abroad work. Joe drove various lorries in the 1960s, included a Scania 110 fleet number C56 registration FLK 287J. In the 1980s Joe had a DAF 2800 C46 registration VMK329J.
Joe's nickname was 'Cowboy Curtis' Joe loved Country music and often did some singing along with 'Handsome Jack', accompanied by 'Yorkie' on the guitar.
Joe finished at Crow Carrying in 1985. He now lives in Spain. Joe was also one of Crow's 'Magnificent Seven'.

Joe with Scania C56

Joe with Scania C56

Joe with D.A.F C46

Photos courtesy of Terry Edwards

Crow Carrying Co Ltd Drivers Profile Les Rudgley 1968 - 1985

Les joined Crow Carrying in 1968, just at the time when Crows moved premises from Barking to Silvertown. Les was on general work and abroad work. The contract work he undertook is however not known. Unfortunately, the lorries which Les drove are also unknown, but the last lorry he drove for Crows was a DAF 2800 C105 registration EHK 957Y.
When Les left the firm he ended up driving for Gussions.

Photos courtesy of Terry Edwards

Les Rudgley. D.A.F 2800 C105 in workshop

Les Rudgley

Joe Curtis & Les Rudgley

Les Rudgley. D.A.F 2800 C105 in workshop

Crow Carrying Co Ltd Drivers Profile Albert Fowler 1965 - 1970s

Albert Fowler joined Crow Carrying in 1965. Albert was known as 'Chicken Fowler'. He held various types of jobs with Crows. Although on general work with his Scania 80 fleet C174. He had also done abroad work to Italy, Switzerland and Germany. He also drove a Volvo F88. He is pictured below in Italy with his son Darren Fowler. He finished at Crows in late 1970s.

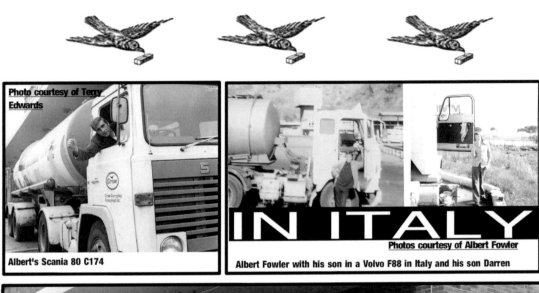

Photo courtesy of Terry Edwards

Albert's Scania 80 C174

IN ITALY

Photos courtesy of Albert Fowler

Albert Fowler with his son in a Volvo F88 in Italy and his son Darren

Albert's Scania 80 C174 at Berger Paints

Photo courtesy of Terry Edwards

Crow Carrying Co Ltd Drivers Profile Ernest Sutherland
1968 - 1985

Ernie joined Crow Carrying in 1968. Prior to this he worked for the Pickford Tanker firm. He got the job with Crows through one of his mates.

The trucks he drove were various Scammells, a Volvo F86, and a DAF 2800 fleet C 99. He also test drove a Scammell Crusader, of which there was only one.

The contract Ernie worked on was LDF, he also did abroad work, that's where he got his nickname, 'Ernie shitbag'.

Ernie saw the end of the Barking depot when Crows moved to Silvertown in 1969.

When Ernie finished in 1985 he went on to drive for Calor Transport and LPG Transport then TDG where he eventually retired.

Ernie drove this Scammell Crusader on test 1970

Ernie drove drove   D.A.F 2800 C99   1984-85   Photo courtesy of pm photography

Crow Carrying Co Ltd Drivers Profile 1968 - 1985

James Lorryman joined Crow Carrying in 1968. He was on general work and contract work to Tate & Lyle, Mars Chocolate, Vandenberg & Jergons and Berks Acids.
The lorries James drove were a Scammell Handyman unknown fleet number, a Volvo F86 fleet number unknown and a Blue Scania 110 fleet unknown.
Jimmy's last lorry was a DAF 2800 fleet 96. Jimmy drove three similar lorries to those in the photographs below.

Photo courtesy of pm photography

Photo courtesy of pm photography

Photo courtesy of Terry Edwards

This is Jimmy Lorrymans
last lorry on Crow's
DAF 2800 Fleet 96

Photo courtesy of Terry Edwards

Photo courtesy of Terry Edwards

Crow Carrying Co Ltd Drivers Profile John Godwin 1970 - 1985

John worked on the Union Carbide contract in Hythe .Crows had the contract for years John started in 1970 and Crows lost the contract in 1975 and opened southampton depot. We would work out of Silvertown on local all week and then back to Southampton depot at the weekend.
 in 1985 they shut the depot and John went on Calor. The lorries he drove were various
including the lorries below The DAF 2800 bottom right hand corner was taken at the Southhampton depot

Photos courtesy of John Godwin

John's Volvo F86 C41

John's Volvo F86 C105

John's Volvo F86 C41

John's Volvo F86 C105

Crow Carrying Co Ltd Drivers Profile Dan Carey 1971 - 1980

Dan joined Crow Carrying in 1971, driving a Scammel Handyman, progressing to a AEC Mandator, Seddon Atkinson, a Foden, an Atkinson Borderer, a Volvo, and a Scania.

Dan remembers the AEC Mandator as a C27 and the Seddon Atkinson was a C22. I was on Tate & Lyle and Esso Chemical mainly, but did a lot of general work before that. I had a C27 which kept splitting its chassis and had to it plated a few times, another time while driving down the M1 the governors packed up, it got faster and faster so he had to hold it back with the engine stop button.

He finished working for Crow Carrying around 1980 after about 9 years.

Photo courtesy of pm photography

Scammell Handyman

Scania   Photo courtesy of pm photography

Foden   Photo courtesy of Terry Edwards

GMM 352N

Crow Carrying Co Ltd Drivers Profile Fred Storehouse
1973 - 1985

Fred worked for Thomas Allan Ltd, before joining Crow Carrying. Fred got the job through his wife, who at the time, worked as the contracts secretary. He was on general work and on contract work for P&G and some abroad work.

Fred drove various lorries, but one that came to mind is a Volvo F86 C165, which was on contract to P&G and passed down from Phil Hartwell.

Fred also drove a Seddon Atkinson passed down from Freddy Crain. Fred also had a DAF 2800 C108. He was on contract to P&G out of the Manchester depot, which had a container tank. Fred's son also worked at Crows in the late 1980s until the finish in 1985, just like his father.

Fred ended up on TDG, which was really Crows, he retired in 2001.

Fred said there was two good tanker firms around Thomas Allen & Crows.

Heres Fred Stonehouse cooking his breakfast next to his Vovlo F86 C165 abroad 1973   **Photos courtesy of Terry Edwards**

Freds DAF 2800 C108 container tank on contract for P&G 1982   **Photos courtesy of Terry Edwards**

Crow Carrying Co Ltd Drivers Profile Tommy Pennington
1974 - 1978

Tommy worked for Harold Wood prior to joining Crow Carrying in 1974. Tommy started at the Widnes depot. The lorries he drove were a C48 Scammell Handyman registration AYN209H, an Atkinson Borderer C202 an C238 ERF A Series registration TMT349M, and a C54 DAF 2800 registration FNO579T. All from the Widnes depot.

Tommy was on contract work to P&G but mostly on general work, he did go abroad but not often.

Tommy finished at Crows and joined Tankfreight. then went to work for Gussions.

His final comment about Crows was, it was the best job and the best bunch of lads to work with.

C235 Pictured here ERF A Series similar to C238 Which was Tommy Penningtons lorry

C54 DAF 2800 reg FNO579T   Photo courtesy of Tommy Pennington

C54 DAF 2800 reg FNO579T   Photo courtesy of Tommy Pennington

Crow Carrying Co Ltd Drivers Profile Kenny Charnick
1980 - 1985

Kenny joined Crow Carrying in 1980 through Gary Smith, one of the Managers at Thomas Allen Ltd, for whom he then worked. Kenny also worked for Tankfreight, Calor Transport and then the oil rigs.
Kenny was mostly on general work he also was on contract to Tate & Lyle Sugars, and whilst travelled abroad.
The lorries he drove were a Volvo F88 fleet 26 registration TMG 728S, a Seddon Atkinson 400 Fleet 36 registration RME 58R, a Volvo F7 Fleet 74 registration GMC 293V.
After Crow Carrying Company folded he joined Wincanton and various other firms.

Kenny's Volvo F88 Fleet C38

Photo courtesy of
Kenny Charnick

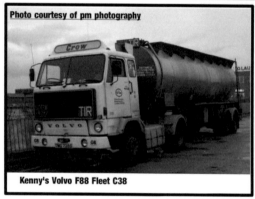

Photo courtesy of pm photography

Kenny's Volvo F88 Fleet C38

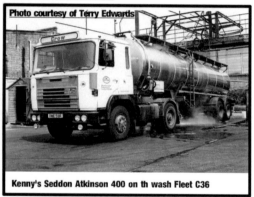

Photo courtesy of Terry Edwards

Kenny's Seddon Atkinson 400 on th wash Fleet C36

Photo courtesy of Terry Edwards

Kenny's Volvo F7 Fleet C74 simlar to this one

Crow Carrying Co Ltd Drivers Profile Brian Wylde 1980 - 1985

Brian joined Crow Carrying in 1980. Prior to this Brian worked for Thomas Allen Ltd. He came to Crows through Gary Smith one of Thomas Allen Ltd Managers at the time.
In 1980 he mostly was on general work but he also did contract work to Tate & Lyle Sugars.
The lorries he drove were a Volvo F88 fleet unknown and a Volvo F7 Fleet 74 registration GMC 293V.
After Crow Carrying Company folded he went to LPG then various other firms including DCL

Brian's Volvo F88 Fleet unknown   **Photos courtesy of Terry Edwards**

Brians Volvo F7 Fleet C74   **Photos courtesy of Terry Edwards**

Crow Carrying Co Ltd Drivers Profile Clifford Stimson
1980 - 1985

Cliff joined Crow Carrying in 1980. When he told Jack Browning 'handsome Jack', another driver at Crows, that he was between jobs, Jack told him to try Crow Carrying, which he did and started with them on the Monday. Cliff did general work for Crows carrying Pebro's Chocolate and Tunnel Glucose.
The lorries he drove were a Scammell Handyman Fleet number unknown, a Volvo F88 fleet unknown, a Guy fleet unknown, Volvo F7 fleet C73 and a Seddon Atkinson fleet 95.
When Crow Carrying folded in 1985, he eventually went to TDG

Heres Cliff Stimson with he's Cadalac and behind he's Volvo F7 C73   **Photos courtesy of Clifford Stimson**
and next to it the last one he had was a Seddon Atkinson C95

Photos courtesy of Terry Edwards

Crow Carrying Co Ltd Drivers Profile Micky Walsh 1981 - 1985

Micky worked for Thomas Allen before joining Crow Carrying. Micky came to Crows through Gary Smith, who was a Manager at Thomas Allen. Micky was on general work and mostly spent time working on the Tate & Lyle Contract.
The lorries Micky drove were a Scania 110, a Guy Big J, a Seddon Atkinson with a day cab then a Volvo F7. Micky's last lorry was a DAF 2800 C39, which became the first Crow lorry to be painted in Buckley Tankers colours, when they took over from Crow Carrying in 1985.
Micky finished in 1985 and went back to drive for Thomas Allen.

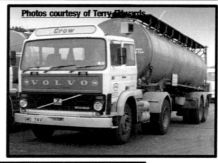

Crow Carrying Co Ltd Drivers Profile Richard Bailey 1984 - 1985

Richard Bailey otherwise known as Dick started working for Crow Carrying in 1984, prior to this Dick was a driver for Harris Coaches & Haulage.
Dick found himself out of work for a while so he decided to make a visit to Crow Carrying Company and ask for a job. He got a job and while there he was on oil trades for Petro Fina, he drove a F7 Volvo.
When Crows folded in 1985 he joined Tankfreight then .When DHL took over he was on the BP Air contract until he retired.

Dick drove simlar Volvo's to these ones on Petrofina contract   Photo courtesy of Terry Edwards

Photo courtesy of pm photography

My Personal Memories of Crow Carrying Co Ltd 1964 - 1985

These are my personal memories of Crow Carrying Company. My father, Robert York nicknamed 'Yorkie', first lifted me up into a Scammell Highwayman when I was just over a year old strapping me in with rags. The Scammell he drove was a C112. I remember very early mornings and a lot of waiting around when loading and unloading. I also remember him having a Scammell Highwayman 111 C86. In the Scammell I recall how the gate change gear box looked just like a maze.

My father also drove a Leyland Beaver C115, then a AEC Mandator C27, which was very fast, they were my favourite lorries of the 1960s. He was issued a Scammell Handyman C141. In those early days I recall him being away from home for over three months at a time, that was when the 'Magnificent Seven' started. The drivers ran the work how they wanted to, but more about that later. Crows stopped buying the Scammells and switched to the Swedish lorries like Scanias and Volvos. My father was issued with a Scania 110 C102, it was far better than he had before, more comfort and much quieter. He then got a DAF 2800 C44, which was even better. I recall going over to Holland and Germany. with my father

One day he was due to go to Italy, so we left for Dover, it was raining and he drove in to the dock and waved to the man in the office. I could see we were getting closer to the only lorry in the lorry park, I shouted at him to watch out, but it was no good he hit it. I really don't think he wanted to go to Italy. The last lorry my father drove for Crows was a DAF 2800 C104.

Finally, when arriving at work one morning in 1985, he was told along with the rest of the work force, that they were being made redundant. My father couldn't believe it, and he said to me the good old days are gone.

This is a panoramic view of silvertown depot taken from my cine 8 film put on stills from 1979

Photos courtesy of pm photography

These two Scammells are simlar to what my dad drove

My dad's parked Crow Tanker at home 1968

Gate change gear box looked like a maze

Crow Carrying Co Ltd on Contract

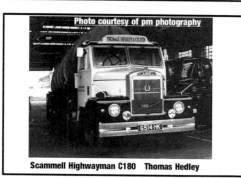

Scammell Highwayman C180   Thomas Hedley

GMC C54 Anglo-Dutch Petroleum Co

Scammell C113 Hercules

Scammell C68 BP

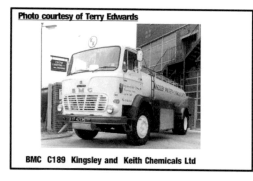

BMC C189 Kingsley and Keith Chemicals Ltd

Scammell Chevron

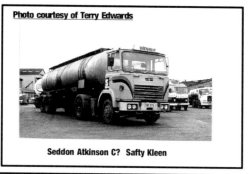

Seddon Atkinson C? Safty Kleen

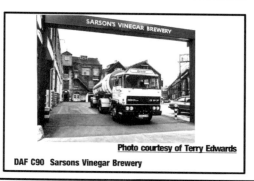

DAF C90 Sarsons Vinegar Brewery

Crow Carrying Co Ltd - Miscellaneous

Photo courtesy of Mark Crow

Not a original Crow van but customised and owned by Mark Crow hence the name on side of van also number on van is Mark's year of birth

CROW CARRYING CO FLEET, JULY 1970

ARTICS

Atkinson	1
Bedford	14
Commer	3
ERF A-Series	1
AEC Mandator	18
AEC Mercury	13
BMC Mastiff	1
Guy Big J	3
Guy Invincible	1
Guy Warrior	1
Leyland Beaver	8
Leyland Comet	2
Scammell Handyman	97
Scammell Highwayman	41
Scammell Trunker	1
TOTAL	**205**

RIGIDS

Atkinson	6
Bedford	4
AEC Mercury	9
BMC Laird	1
BMC Mastiff	5
Leyland Octopus	1
TOTAL	**26**

Note: Official records do not provide a further breakdown into model names, etc.

Crow Flag

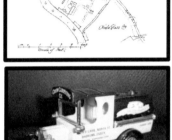

Crow Map of Barking Depot

Crow memorabilia & collectables from top left to right Crow shoe shine kit.Crow Advert. Crow wage slip Crow pen .Crow Badges. Crow Key Ring Crow Pension book Crow Modals crow wallet Crow Astray Crow Overal Badge & clock

Crow Ledo Modal & Cups

Crow D.I.Y Modal

Crow Carrying Co Ltd Front Sign at Barking 1920 - 1945
Photo courtesy of Terry Edwards

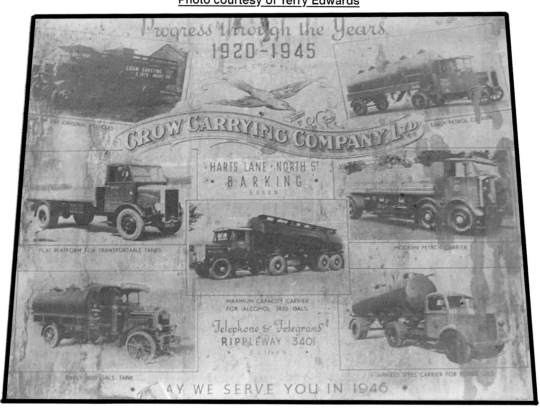

Crow Carrying Co Ltd Advert 1920s

73

Crow Carrying Co Ltd Adverts 1940s to the 1970s

CROW CARRYING COMPANY LTD. 1944

MOTOR HAULAGE CONTRACTORS

ROAD TANKS
OF VARYING CAPACITIES
IN
STAINLESS STEEL
ALUMINIUM
RUBBER LINED
LEAD LINED, Etc.

for the distribution of

EDIBLE AND OTHER
OILS AND CHEMICALS
ALSO VEHICLES OF
ALL TYPES FOR
GENERAL HAULAGE
AVAILABLE ON
CONTRACT OR CASUAL HIRE

RAILWAY SIDING AND WHARF
HARTS LANE, NORTH STREET BARKING, ESSEX

CROW CARRYING COMPANY LTD. 1959

Motor Haulage Contractors

ROAD TANKS
of varying capacities in
STAINLESS STEEL
ALUMINIUM
RUBBER LINED
LEAD LINED, etc.,
for the distribution of
EDIBLE and other
OILS and CHEMICALS
also vehicles of
all types for
GENERAL HAULAGE
available on
Contract or
Casual Hire

for the **TRANSPORT**
of all
BULK LIQUIDS
Harts Lane, North Street, Barking
Tel.: RIPPLEWAY 0366 (4 lines)

Harts Lane, North Street, Barking, Essex

Tel: Rippleway 0366 (4 lines)

Manchester Depot:
231 Greengate, Middleton Junction, Middleton
Manchester. Tel: Failsworth 3353 and 2242

for the
TRANSPORT
of
**BULK LIQUIDS
POWDERS
GASES**

FOR HAULAGE OF

BULK LIQUIDS POWDERS GASES

CROW CARRYING COMPANY LTD.

LONDON

Crescent Wharf
North Woolwich Road,
London, E.16
01-476 3645 (4 lines)
01-476 4231 (3 lines)

MANCHESTER

231 Greengate
Middleton Junction
Manchester
061 FAI 2242 or 3353

Crow Carrying Co Ltd Advert 1960s

Keep your B.M.C. vehicles earning more with

GENUINE PARTS

REPLACEMENT UNITS

FACTORY-TRAINED MECHANICS

TECHNICAL SERVICE

APPROVED ACCESSORIES

SERVICE VOUCHER PLAN

B.M.C. Service comprises a round-the-clock "Vehicle off the Road" Service, expert technical advice which is in the hands of factory-trained mechanics, together with Genuine Parts and Replacement Units covered by the B.M.C. 12 Months' Warranty. You can get this unbeatable Service from your appointed B.M.C. Dealer. It is false economy with vehicles that have got to earn their keep to be satisfied with anything less.

B.M.C. SERVICE LIMITED, Cowley, Oxford

Crow Carrying Co Ltd Advert 1960s
Advert courtesy of Commercial Motor

Directors
F. ROWLAND WALLER, F.C.A.
F. J. REYNOLDS, M.Inst.T., M.I.E.C.
FRED B. CROW
A. T. CROW, B.Sc.

Telephones and
Telegrams :
RIPPLEWAY 0366
(4 lines)

TANK VEHICLES AVAILABLE FOR SERVICE TO AND FROM THE CONTINENT

SPECIALISTS FOR OVER 40 YEARS

in the transportation of Bulk Liquids. Our wide technical experience in the handling and distribution of Bulk Oils, Gases and Chemicals can solve your problems.

HEAD OFFICE :
RAILWAY SIDINGS AND WHARF
HARTS LANE · NORTH STREET
BARKING · ESSEX
TEL : RIPPLEWAY 0366 (4 LINES) P.B.X.

DEPOT:
231 GREENGATE
MIDDLETON
MANCHESTER
FAILSWORTH 3353 & 2242

The Reavell T100 compressor gives you what you want.

A quick turn round.

Reavell compressors and exhausters can 'speed up' the loading and unloading of all types of liquids and powdered or granular solids. These machines can be driven through a power take-off, or by electric or hydraulic motors. They also feature a lubricating oil tank that can be remotely mounted.

With these machines you get another bonus : Reavell reliability.

Further information on Reavell products is available on request.

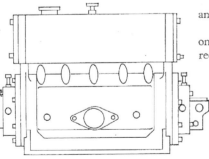

COMPAIR INDUSTRIAL DIVISION

Reavell & Co Ltd Dept K4, Ranelagh Works, Ipswich, IP2 0AE. Telephone: Ipswich 56124. Telex: 98254

Crow Carrying Co Ltd Advert 1970s

Advert courtesy of Transport Journal

Photos curtesy of Terry Edwards

Crow Carrying Co Ltd Advert 1970s

Scania LB110

LB110 (4x2), LBS110 (6x2), LBT110 (6x4).

Scania DS11, 6 cylinder turbocharged. Output 250 hp, torque 723 lb.f.ft. (BS.Au. 141:1 1971) or Scania D11, output 199 hp, torque 571 lb.f.ft. (DIN).

10 speed range change gearbox or 5 speed gearbox. Fully synchronized. Three different rear-axle gears: normal single reduction, hypoid single reduction, single reduction with hub reduction. Double drive bogie on LBT110. Hydraulic power steering, dual-circuit direct-acting fullair brakes, springtype handbrake, safety tilt cab.

Crow Carrying Co Ltd Advert 1980s

NATIONALLY AND INTERNATIONALLY
As the Crow flies . . .

Photograph by courtesy of T. Edwards, Crow Carrying Co. Ltd.

ECONOMICALLY

EFFICIENTLY

CAREFULLY

HAZARDOUS & NON-HAZARDOUS BULK LIQUID MOVEMENTS

For information/quotation
contact:
LONDON
Gary Smith — 01 476 0211. Telex: 896529
HULL
Stuart Pascall — 0482-702274
SOUTHAMPTON
Cyril Hillier — 0703-736011

CROW

CARRYING

COMPANY LTD

Crow Carrying Co Ltd Advert 1980s

Advert courtesy of Truck magazine and photos Terry Edwards

As the Crow flies...

The Crow Carrying Company Limited have again purchased Volvo F7's for their specialised bulk liquid services through-out the UK and Europe.

These were supplied by Rydale Trucks Limited to comply with Petroleum Regulation standards.

Crow chose Volvo F7's for the following reasons:
* Economy
* Reliability
* Maximum payload capacity
* Driver acceptance.

So when it comes to delivering the goods, Volvo rolls... as the CROW flies.

rydale trucks

THE VOLVO LONDON TRUCK CENTRE
47 Sewardstone Road, Chingford, London E4 7PU.
Telephone 01-529 8686.

Photographs by courtesy of Terence Edwards.
Crow Carrying Company Limited.

Crow Carrying Co Ltd Drivers Gallery through the Years

Crow employees on a outing to the South Coast 1940s 50s

Crow workshop staff names unknown? 1940s or 50s?

Driver Harold Grosvenor and family & A.E.C.C27 1950s
Photo courtesy of Steve Grovner

Photos courtesy of Terry Edwards

Crow drivers waiting for work.John Snooks Bobby York Jack Browning & Alan Huish 1980s

Crow Carrying Co Ltd Drivers Gallery through the Years

Mick Hall & Kay Wilson Tea Lady
Jimmy Collins   Photos courtesy of
                Terry Edwards

Jeff Braithwaite

Peter Reeves Genral Manager

Jackie Court

Scammell C62

Bert Butt

Jeff Braithwaite
Dave Bennett

Alfred Liddard Harry Power Jackie Barnfield Ernie
Sutherland Alexander Wilkins

?   Cyrill Hillier   ?

Teddy Battman in DAF
C91

C71   Unknown Driver

Albert Harris & Larry Lythal

Crow Carrying Co Ltd Fleet List 1-14

leet	Reg plate	Truck name 1	Truck name 2	Truck type	Contract	Driver	Photo
1	XA9036	THORNYCROFT J		4+2 sided			X
1	445 LTW	SCAMMELL	Highwayman	4+2MU	Geigy		X
2	XA9045	THORNYCROFT J		4+2 sided			X
2	YPU 753	SCAMMELL	Highwayman	4+2 MU	ABRAC		X
2	HPU 226	BEDFORD		4+2 Tank	ICI		X
2	4589PV	SCAMMELL	Highwayman	4+2 MU	Carbide		X
2	SGP 341F	LEYLAND	Beaver	4+2 MU			
2	LMT 551P	GUY	Big J	4+2 MU			
3		LEYLAND	Hippo	6+4 Tank			X
3	LPV 188	SCAMMELL	Highwayman	4+2 MU			
3	8851PU	SCAMMELL	Highwayman	4+2 MU			
4	LWC 190	LEYLAND	Comet	4+2 MU			X
4	ATW 481	LEYLAND	Comet	4+2 MU			
4	WYX 703G	SCAMMELL	Highwayman	4+2 MU			
5	EEV 82	BEDFORD		4+2 sided			
5	KGJ878K	GUY	Big J	4+2 MU			X
6	LMU 469P	GUY	Big J	4+2 MU			
6	YVX 141	SCAMMELL	Highwayman	4+2 MU			X
7	JNO 153	SCAMMELL	Highwayman	4+2 MU			
7	1521F	SCAMMELL	Highwayman	4+2 MU		Jack Threshie	X
7	WYK 698G	SCAMMELL	Highwayman	4+2 MU			
8		AEC	Monarch	4+2 Tank	Tar Diistillers		X
8	953 NVX	SCAMMELL	Highwayman	4+2 MU			X
8	ONO 886	LEYLAND	Comet	4+2 MU			X
8	XYV621H	SCAMMELL	Handyman	4+2 MU			X
9	PVW 518	SCAMMELL	Highwayman	4+2 MU			X
9		BEDFORD		4+2 MU			X
10	SCG 445F	SCAMMELL	Handyman	4+2 MU			
10	XGO 207G	SCAMMELL	Handyman	4+2 MU			
10	VHK438	SCAMMELL	Highwayman	4+2 MU			X
10	GNO 161	LEYLAND	Hippo	6+4 Tank			X
11	OO4389	SCAMMELL	Highwayman	4+2 MU	L+N		X
11	JPU 975	SCAMMELL	Highwayman	4+2 MU			X
11	TW 513	AEC	701	4+2 MU			X
11	725PNO	AUSTIN		4+2 Tank			X
12	HPO 819B	SCAMMELL	Handyman	4+2 MU			
12	ONO 887	SCAMMELL	Highwayman	4+2 MU		Alf Tucker	X
13	NGO 205G	SCAMMELL	Highwayman	4+2 MU			
13	HDO 274	FORDSON		4+2 Tank			X
13	727 PNO	AUSTIN		4+2 Tank			X
13	OMC 256R	SEDDON ATKIN 400		4+2 MU			
14	OHK 30	SCAMMELL	Highwayman	4+2 MU			
14	NMC 354R	SEDDON ATKIN 400		4+2 MU			X
14	SGP 51F	LEYLAND	Beaver	4+2 MU			

Crow Carrying Co Ltd Fleet List 15-29

leet	Reg plate	Truck name 1	Truck name 2	Truck type	Contract	Driver	Photo
15	Kev 206	SCAMMELL	Highwayman	4+2 MU			
15	8949F	SCAMMELL	Highwayman	4+2 MU	L+N		X
15	XYY 622H	SCAMMELL	Handyman	4+2 MU			
16	JD4896	BEDFORD	OW	4+2 Van			X
16	KEV 204	BEDFORD	O	4+2 Tank			
16	VTW11	BEDFORD		4+2 Tank			X
17	KNO 234	SCAMMELL	Highwayman	4+2 MU			
17	VOO 959	AEC	Mercury	4+2 Tank			X
17	KNO 224	AEC		4+2 Tank			
17	XYY 717G	SCAMMELL	Highwayman 3	4+2 MU			
17	XYY 631H	SCAMMELL	Handyman	4+2 MU			
18	NMC 149R	SEDDON ATKIN	400	4+2 MU			
18	SOC 446F	LEYLAND	Beaver	4+2 MU			X
18	VTW12	SCAMMELL	Highwayman	4+2 MU			
19	UV5009	SCAMMELL	Highwayman	4+2 MU		Jack Threshie	X
19	WYX 689G	SCAMMELL	Handyman	4+2 MU		Phil Hartwell	X
19	KEV 962	SCAMMELL	Highwayman	4+2 MU			X
20	TMT 406M	VOLVO	F88	4+2 MU			
20	NVX 406	SCAMMELL	Highwayman	4+2 MU		Lidard	X
21	327 PVW	SCAMMELL	Highwayman	4+2 MU	Malt Vinegar		X
22	RNO 538	SCAMMELL	Highwayman	4+2 MU			
22	XGO 197G	SCAMMELL	Handyman	4+2 MU			X
22	NMC 195R	SEDDON ATKIN	400	4+2 MU			X
23	YW2 706	AEC		4+2 Sided			X
23	SGP56P	AEC	Mandator	4+2 MU			X
23	XTW 419	SCAMMELL	Highwayman	4+2 MU			
23	NMC 566R	SEDDON ATKIN	400	4+2 MU			X
24	EYW 82	SCAMMELL	Highwayman	4+2 MU			
24	448 9HK	SCAMMELL	Highwayman	4+2 MU			
24	AYF 466H	SCAMMELL	Handyman	4+2 MU			X
24	NMC 644R	SEDDON ATKIN	400	4+2 MU	Hercules		X
25	YHK 959	SCAMMELL	Highwayman	4+2 MU		John Smith	X
25	UML 437F	AEC	Mandator	4+2 MU			X
25	GNO 70	LEYLAND	Lynx	4+2Flat			X
25		SEDDON ATKIN	400	4+2 MU			X
26	EH1 452	AEC		4+2 Tank			
26	XTW 482	SCAMMELL	Highwayman	4+2 MU			
26	WYX 681G	SCAMMELL	Handyman	4+2 MU			X
27	OPU 551	AEC	MONARCH	4+2 Tank			X
27	VW 431	AEC		4+2 Tank			
27	UMX 106F	AEC	MANDATOR	4+2 MU			X
28	1522F	AEC	MERCURY	4+2 Tank			X
28		BEDFORD		4+2 Tank			
28	WYX 711G	SCAMMELL	Handyman	4+2 MU			X
29	JVW851	SCAMMELL	Highwayman	4+2 MU			X

Crow Carrying Co Ltd Fleet List 29-41

leet	Reg plate	Truck name 1	Truck name 2	Truck type	Contract	Driver	Photo
29	VW2800	SCAMMELL	CHAIN DRIVE	4+2 MU			X
29	NMC971R	VOLVO	F88	4+2 MU			
30	WPV498	SCAMMELL	Highwayman	4+2 MU			
30	JPU939	INTERNATIONAL		4+2 Tank			
30	VX835	LEYLAND		4+2 Tank			
30	OLC 410L	ATKINSON	borderer	4+2 MU			
30	XGW 353F	LEYLAND	Beaver	4+2 MU			X
30	RME 571R	VOLVO	F86	4+2 MU			X
31	OLC 419L	ATKINSON	Borderer	4+2 MU			X
31	XTW 483	LEYLAND	Comet	4+2 MU			
31	MOO74	SCAMMELL	Highwayman	4+2 MU			
32	HGY 634C	SCAMMELL	Highwayman	4+2 MU			
32	175 FHR	BEDFORD	S Type	4+2 MU			
32	RMG 288R	VOLVO	F88	4+2 MU			X
33	209 FVX	SCAMMELL	Highwayman	4+2 MU			
33	XYV 626H	SCAMMELL	Highwayman	4+2 MU	ICI		X
33	RMG 287R	VOLVO	F88	4+2 MU			X
33	GKX 915	INTERNATIONAL		4+2 Tank			X
34	OLC 420L	ATKINSON	borderer	4+2 MU			X
34	794 UPU	SCAMMELL	Highwayman	4+2 MU			
34	JVW 877	SCAMMELL	Highwayman	4+2 MU			
34	RME 59R	SEDDON ATKINSON		4+2 Tank			X
35	VX4393	SCAMMELL	CHAIN DRIVE	4+2 MU	Texaco		X
35	XGO 204G	SCAMMELL	Handyman	4+2 MU			X
35	YTW 973	SCAMMELL	Highwayman	4+2 MU			X
35	RMG 56R	SEDDON ATKIN	400	4+2 MU			
35	TEV3R	DAF	2300	4+2 MU			X
36	SNO15	SCAMMELL	Highwayman	4+2 MU			
36	RME 58R	SEDDON ATKIN	400	4+2 MU			X
37	SNO17	SCAMMELL	Highwayman	4+2 MU			X
37	SMM 716S	VOLVO	F86	4+2 MU			
38		SCAMMELL	CHAIN DRIVE	4+2 MU			X
38	LVX615	AEC	Monarch	4+2 Tank			X
38	KEV 207	SCAMMELL	Highwayman	4+2 MU			X
38	4381NO	SCAMMELL	Highwayman	4+2 MU			
38	WYX 694G	SCAMMELL	Handyman	4+2 MU			
38		VOLVO	F88	4+2 MU			X
39	CVW615	AEC		4+2 Tank			X
39	VHK 439	BEDFORD	S Type	4+2 Tank			
40	SGP343F	AEC	Mandator	4+2 MU			X
40	OHK31	SCAMMELL	Highwayman	4+2 MU			X
41	OHK32	AEC		4+2 Tank			
41	ANO 733	MORRIS COMMER		4+2 Van			
41	XBY 841G	AEC	Mandator	4+2 MU			
41	WTW 336	AEC	Mercury	4+2 Tank	ICI		X

Crow Carrying Co Ltd Fleet List 41-54

leet	Reg plate	Truck name 1	Truck name 2	Truck type	Contract	Driver	Photo
41		VOLVO	F86	4+2 MU			
42	WYX 691	SCAMMELL	Handyman	4+2 MU			
42	ANO734	MORRIS COMMER		4+2 Van			X
42	AVW728	SCAMMELL	Highwayman	4+2 MU			
42	TMP13S	SEDDON ATKIN	400	4+2 MU			X
43		SCAMMELL	6 Ton Mech Hor	4+2 MU	British Vinegar	Bill Moor	X
43	7508 NO	ATKINSON	borderer	8+4 Tank			X
43	XGO202	AEC	Mandator	4+2 MU			
43	VMG 370S	DAF	2800	4+2 MU			X
44	MUU 478D	BEDFORD		4+2 MU			X
44	LVX41	SCAMMELL	Highwayman	4+2 MU			
44	VMG 371S	DAF	2800	4+2 MU		Rob York	X
45	7571NO	SCAMMELL	Highwayman	4+2 MU			X
45	XYK 879G	SCAMMELL	Handyman	4+2 MU			
46	VMK 329S	DAF	2800	4+2 MU		Joe Curtis	X
46	BPU19	LEYLAND	Badger	4+2 Tank			X
46	SNO16	SCAMMELL	Highwayman	4+2 MU			X
47		SCAMMELL	Highwayman	4+2 MU			
47	XGO 198G	SCAMMELL	Handyman	4+2 MU			
47	PEV639	SCAMMELL	Highwayman	4+2 MU			
47	VMK 345S	DAF	2800	4+2 MU		Alf Lidard	X
48	478CPU	BEDFORD	S TYPE	4+2 MU			
48		SCAMMELL	Highwayman	4+2 MU			
48	AYN 209H	SCAMMELL	Handyman	4+2 MU			
48	JMF23N	VOLVO	F88	4+2 MU			X
49	ONO212	ALBION	Clydsdale	4+2 Tank			X
49		AEC	Monarch	4+2 Tank			
49	LWC191	BEDFORD	O	4+2 MU			X
49	WVX188	LEYLAND	Comet	4+2 MU			X
49	WML30T	DAF	2800	4+2 MU		Jackie Barnfield	X
50	OLC410	ATKINSON	borderer	4+2 MU	CTW		X
50	OHK432	AEC		4+2 Tank			
51	JHK2	SCAMMELL	Highwayman	4+2 MU			X
51	4490HK	SCAMMELL	Highwayman	4+2 MU			
52	OTW 410S	SCAMMELL	Highwayman	4+2 MU			
52	XYK 873G	SCAMMELL	Handyman	4+2 MU		Albert Harris	X
52	WML 210T	DAF	2500	4+2 MU	L+N		X
52	GUL78J	SCANIA	110	4+2 MU			X
53	VVW873	LEYLAND	Comet	4+2 MU			X
54	28BWC	LEYLAND	Comet	4+2 MU	Geigy		X
54		GMC		4+2 Tank	A.D Petroleum Co		X
54		LEYLAND	Hippo	6+4 Tank			
54	689FPV	BEDFORD	S TYPE	4+2 MU			
54	FMO579T	DAF	2800	4+2 MU			X
54	OGW 856K	ATKINSON	borderer	4+2 MU			

Crow Carrying Co Ltd Fleet List 55-71

leet	Reg plate	Truck name 1	Truck name 2	Truck type	Contract	Driver	Photo
55	JNO778	SCAMMELL	Highwayman	4+2 MU			
55	1523F	SCAMMELL	Highwayman	4+2 MU		John Smith	X
55	WML 405T	DAF	2500	4+2 MU		Jackie Barnfield	X
56	FLK 287J	SCANIA	110	4+2 MU		Joe Curtis	X
56	176FHK	BEDFORD	A	4+2 MU			
57	885FWC	LEYLAND	Comet	4+2 MU			
57	OLC 408L	ATKINSON	borderer	4+2 MU			X
58	XEV814	LEYLAND		4+2 MU			
58	VOO962	LEYLAND	Comet	4+2 MU			X
58	HME 765N	ATKINSON	borderer	4+2 MU			X
59	OGW 357K	ATKINSON	borderer	4+2 MU			X
59	KPU808	SCAMMELL	Highwayman	4+2 MU			X
60	950NEV	SCAMMELL	Highwayman	4+2 MU	Geigy		X
61	701YOO	SCAMMELL	Highwayman	4+2 MU			
61	MEV718	SCAMMELL	Highwayman	4+2 MU			X
61	OLC412L	ATKINSON	borderer	4+2 MU			
61	CMT 857V	VOLVO	F7	4+2 MU			
62	MNO13	AEC		4+2 Tank			
62	XYV629H	SCAMMELL	Handyman	4+2 MU		Burt Butt	X
63	7509NC	ATKINSON	borderer	8+4Tank			
63	149ANO	SCAMMELL	R8	8+4Tank			
63	WYX 683G	SCAMMELL	Handyman	4+2 MU			X
64	MNO7	AEC		4+2 Tank			
64	UMG 593H	VOLVO	F86	4+2 MU			
64	DMT 62V	SEDDON ATKIN	400	4+2 MU			X
65	OLC 421L	ATKINSON	borderer	4+2 MU			X
65	LVX865	SCAMMELL	Highwayman	4+2 MU			
65	OLC 409L	SEDDON ATKIN	400	4+2 MU			
66	WVK 700G	SCAMMELL	Handyman	4+2 MU			
66	OO9835	LEYLAND	Comet	4+2 MU			X
66	LVX841	SCAMMELL	Highwayman	4+2 MU			
66	DMT 274V	VOLVO	F7	4+2 MU			
67	NEV703	AEC		4+2 Tank			
67	VOO960	AEC		4+2 Tank			X
67	DMT 273V	VOLVO	F7	4+2 MU			
68	210FVX	SCAMMELL	Highwayman	4+2 MU			X
68	AYF 463H	SCAMMELL	Handyman	4+2 MU	BP		X
69	367SOO	SCAMMELL	Highwayman	4+2 MU	L+N	Harry Riley	X
69	MTW481	SCAMMELL	Highwayman	4+2 MU			X
70	LTW419	SCAMMELL	Highwayman	4+2 MU			X
70	TMT 461M	VOLVO	F88	4+2 MU			
70	703YOO	SCAMMELL	Highwayman	4+2 MU	Malt Vinegar		X
71	EHK978	SCAMMELL	Highwayman	4+2 MU			
71	GMF351N	VOLVO	F88	4+2 MU			X
71	NPU717	AEC		4+2 Tank			

Crow Carrying Co Ltd Fleet List 72-84

leet	Reg plate	Truck name 1	Truck name 2	Truck type	Contract	Driver	Photo
72	PVX504	ALBION	Clydsdale	4+2 Tank			
72	AYF469Y	SCAMMELL	Handyman	4+2 MU			X
72	538VX	SCAMMELL	Highwayman	4+2 MU			X
73	ATM133H	SCAMMELL	Handyman	4+2 MU			
73	JXB342	DENNIS	HORLA	4+2 MU		Charlie Hawkbe	X
73	YNO643	BEDFORD	S TYPE	4+2 MU			
73	KOO396	BEDFORD	TK	4+2 MU			
73		VOLVO	F7	4+2 MU			X
74	NHK568	MAUDSLAY	MOGUL	4+2 Tank	British Vinegars		X
74	2417EV	SCAMMELL	Highwayman	4+2 MU			X
74	AYN 134H	SCAMMELL	Handyman	4+2 MU			X
74	FLK288K	SCANIA	110	4+2 MU			
74	GMC 293V	VOLVO	F7	4+2 MU			X
75	XGX 673E	AEC	Mandator	4+2 MU			
75	GMC 294V	VOLVO	F7	4+2 MU			X
75		SCAMMELL	Highwayman	4+2 MU			
75		BEDFORD		4+2 Tank			
76	3698OO	SCAMMELL	Highwayman	4+2 MU			
76	NPU716	SCAMMELL	Highwayman	4+2 MU			X
77	GVX 190B	COMMER	TS3	4+2 Tank			X
77	NPU717	AEC		4+2 Tank			
77	FLK 288J	SCANIA	110	4+2 MU		Harry Riley	X
77	HMU 163W	VOLVO	F7	4+2 MU			X
78	NVX70	AEC	Monarch	4+2 Tank			X
78	AYM 135H	SCAMMELL	Highwayman	4+2 MU			X
78	KOO797	BEDFORD	TK	4+2 Tank			
78	HMU 256W	VOLVO	F7	4+2 MU			X
79	NPU718	SCAMMELL	Highwayman	4+2 MU			X
79		SCAMMELL	Highwayman	4+2 MU			
79	DLC 412L	ATKINSON	borderer	4+2 MU			X
79	HMU 250W	VOLVO	F7	4+2 MU			X
80	650VVW	COMMER-BMC		4+2 Van			
80	FLC779J	SCANIA	110	4+2 MU			
80	7232NO	MORRIS		4+2 Van			
80	TMT 438M	ATKINSON	borderer	4+2 MU			
80	HMU 249W	VOLVO	F7	4+2 MU			X
81	827AEV	BEDFORD	S TYPE	4+2 MU			
81	UMX 111F	AEC	Mandator	4+2 MU			X
81	HMF 766N	ATKINSON	borderer	4+2 MU			
81	CMT867V	VOLVO	F7	4+2 MU			
82	6791EV	SCAMMELL	Highwayman	4+2 MU			X
83	NVX73	SCAMMELL	Highwayman	4+2 MU			
83	808XWC	SCAMMELL	Highwayman	4+2 MU			X
83	STW 362W	DAF	2800	4+2 MU			
84	RYK948E	SCAMMELL	Handyman	4+2 MU			X

Crow Carrying Co Ltd Fleet List 84-99

leet	Reg plate	Truck name 1	Truck name 2	Truck type	Contract	Driver	Photo
84	OTW179	AEC	Monarch	4+2 Tank			
85	PVX637	ALBION	Clydsdale	4+2 Tank			
85	OLC 413L	ATKINSON	borderer	4+2 MU		Gus Gascoin	X
85	HOO105	SCAMMELL	Highwayman	4+2 MU			
85	CMT 867V	ATKINSON		4+2 MU			
86	HDP 438W	DAF	2800	4+2 MU			
86	PV537	ALBION	Clydsdale	4+2 Tank			
86	T.P	THORNYCROFT		4+2 B.down			X
87	KEV 847C	BEDFORD	TK	4+2 MU			X
87	713BPU	BEDFORD	S TYPE	4+2 MU	Hercules		X
88	MLW 676D	SCAMMELL	Highwayman	4+2 MU			X
88	PHK863	LEYLAND	Comet	4+2 Tank			X
89	6663EV	AEC	Mercury	4+2 Tank			X
89	ATM 136H	SCAMMELL	Handyman	4+2 MU			
90	URK 501F	LEYLAND	Beaver	4+2 MU			
90	PTW24	SCAMMELL	Highwayman	4+2 MU			
90	UHK 211W	DAF	2300	4+2 MU	Sarsons Vinega	Johnny Caygil	X
91	9961K	SCAMMELL	Highwayman	4+2 MU	L+N		X
91	UHK 212W	DAF	2300	4+2 MU	Sarsons Vinega	Teddy Battman	X
92	GUL76J	SCANIA	110	4+2 MU			
92	PVX507	ALBION	Clydsdale	4+2 Tank			
92	7153PU	AEC	Mercury	4+2 Tank			X
93	AYM 137H	SCAMMELL	Handyman	4+2 MU			
93	PVX508	ALBION	Clydsdale	4+2 Tank			X
93	UHK 213W	DAF	2800	4+2 MU			
94	PVX535	ALBION	Clydsdale	4+2 Tank			
94	896UVX	AEC	Mercury	4+2 Tank			X
94	OLM 526W	SEDDON ATKIN	400	4+2 MU			X
94	AVO97X	DAF	2800	4+2 MU			
95	PVX596	ALBION	Clydsdale	4+2 Tank			X
95	VOO963	AEC	Mercury	4+2 Tank			X
95	FLK 285J	SCANIA	110	4+2 MU		Jack Browning	X
95	GLM 527W	SEDDON ATKIN	400	4+2 MU			
96	PTW778	SCAMMELL	Highwayman	4+2 MU			X
96	KRX 861W	DAF	2800	4+2 MU			X
97	KEV 948C	COMMER	TS3	4+2 MU			
97	6358NO	MORRIS		4+2 MU			X
97	NMD903X	VOLVO	F7	4+2 MU			X
98	FWC 823C	AEC	Mercury	4+2 Tank			
98	PTW776	SCAMMELL	Highwayman	4+2 MU			X
99	RTW915	AEC	Monarch	4+2 Tank			X
99	TEV384	AEC	Mercury	4+2 Tank			
99	WYX 709G	SCAMMELL	Handyman	4+2 MU			X
99	2032EV	AEC	Mercury	4+2 Tank			
99	AOO97X	DAF	2800	4+2 MU		Eernie suvalan	X

Crow Carrying Co Ltd Fleet List 100-120

leet	Reg plate	Truck name 1	Truck name 2	Truck type	Contract	Driver	Photo
100	RTW916	SCAMMELL	Highwayman	4+2 MU			X
100	BAM???	SCAMMELL	Highwayman	4+2 MU			
101	5650EV	MORRIS		4+2 MU		Ray Oliff	X
102	TEV610	BEDFORD	S TYPE	4+2 MU			
102	KGH 744K	SCANIA	110	4+2 MU		Rob York	X
102	CEV 210X	DAF	2800	4+2 MU		Roger Walsh	X
103	UMG 680M	VOLVO	F86	4+2 MU			
103	TEV385	SCAMMELL	Highwayman	4+2 MU			
103	AYM 142H	SCAMMELL	Handyman	4+2 MU			X
104	THK598	SCAMMELL	Highwayman	4+2 MU			
104	EHK 955Y	DAF	2800	4+2 MU		Rob York	X
105	TPU333	SCAMMELL	Highwayman	4+2 MU			X
105	EHK 957Y	DAF	2800	4+2 MU		Les Rudley	X
106	TVW893	SCAMMELL	Highwayman	4+2 MU			
106	6792EV	SCAMMELL	Highwayman	4+2 MU	Caxton		X
106	FHJ58Y	DAF	2800	4+2 MU			X
107		AEC	Monarch	4+2 Tank			X
107	XHK960	SCAMMELL	Highwayman	4+2 MU			
107	LOW9Y	MERC		4+2 MU			
107	KGH 745K	SCANIA	110				
108	TVW892	SCAMMELL	Highwayman	4+2 MU			
108	WYM 707G	SCAMMELL	Handyman	4+2 MU			
108	HEV 401Y	DAF	2800	4+2 MU		Fred Stonhouse	X
109	UML 435F	AEC	Mandator	4+2 MU			X
109	UEV995	BEDFORD	S TYPE	4+2 MU			
110	TVX855	SCAMMELL	Highwayman	4+2 MU			X
110	XGO 206G	SCAMMELL	Handyman	4+2 MU			
110	HHJ 481Y	DAF	2800	4+2 MU		Alex Wilkins	X
111	SGP53F	AEC	Mandator	4+2 MU			X
111	UEV996	SCAMMELL	Highwayman	4+2 MU			
112	UEV997	BEDFORD	S TYPE	4+2 Tank			
112	A508 OKX	RENAULT		4+2 MU		Jack Browning	X
113	XGX675G	SCAMMELL	Handyman	4+2 MU	Hercules		X
113	VHK437	SCAMMELL	Highwayman	4+2 MU			X
114	WNO264	AEC	Mercury	4+2 Tank			
114	KGH 747K	VOLVO	F86	4+2 MU			X
115	SGH 354F	LEYLAND	Beaver	4+2 MU			X
115	VTW13	SCAMMELL	Highwayman	4+2 MU	Malt Vinegar		X
116	6613EV	AEC	Mercury	4+2 Tank			X
117	AYF 461H	SCAMMELL	Handyman	4+2 MU			
117	WVW755	SCAMMELL	Highwayman	4+2 MU	ABRAC	Jackie Barnfiel	X
118	XVX578	BEDFORD	A5	4+2 Tank			X
119	XVX575	SCAMMELL	Highwayman	4+2 MU			
120	87XNO	SCAMMELL	Highwayman	4+2 MU		John Smith	X
120	TMT424M	ERF		4+2 MU			X

Crow Carrying Co Ltd Fleet List 121-144

leet	Reg plate	Truck name 1	Truck name 2	Truck type	Contract	Driver	Photo
121	YNO645	BEDFORD	S TYPE	4+2 MU			
122	RYP780E	GUY	Big J	4+2 MU			
122	YVX142	ATKINSON		8+4 Tank			X
123		AEC	Mandator	4+2 MU			
123	YVX143	SCAMMELL	Highwayman	4+2 MU			X
123	XGO199G	SCAMMELL	Handyman	4+2 MU			
124	YVX144	ATKINSON	borderer	8+4 Tank			
124	TKT 354M	ERF	A Series	4+2 MU			
125	KOO798	BEDFORD	TK	4+2 MU			
126	150ANO	SCAMMELL	Highwayman	4+2 MU			X
126	AYF 464H	SCAMMELL	Handyman	4+2 MU	BP		X
127	WYX 686G	SCAMMELL	Handyman	4+2 MU			
127	151ANO	SCAMMELL	Highwayman	4+2 MU		Mc Cormack	X
128	UML 434F	AEC	Mandator	4+2 MU			
128	42AVW	SCAMMELL	Highwayman	4+2 MU			X
129	43AVW	SCAMMELL	Highwayman	4+2 MU			X
130	URK 502F	AEC	Mandator	4+2 MU			X
130	44AVW	SCAMMELL	Highwayman	4+2 MU			
131	45AVW	SCAMMELL	Highwayman	4+2 MU			
132	AYN 210H	SCAMMELL	Handyman	4+2 MU			
132	714BPV	SCAMMELL	Highwayman	4+2 MU			
133	718BPV	SCAMMELL	Highwayman	4+2 MU			
133	GMM 352N	FODEN		4+2 MU			X
134	UML 436F	AEC	Mandator	4+2 MU			X
134	474CPU	SCAMMELL	Highwayman	4+2 MU			
135	LVH688	SCAMMELL	Handyman	4+2 MU			
136	SGP55F	AEC	Mandator	4+2 MU			X
136	LVH689	SCAMMELL	Highwayman	4+2 MU			
137	WYX 701G	SCAMMELL	Handyman	4+2 MU			
137	769DVW	BEDFORD	S TYPE	4+2 MU			X
138	922CVW	SCAMMELL	Highwayman	4+2 MU			X
139	923CVW	SCAMMELL	Highwayman	4+2 MU			X
139	WYX 680X	SCAMMELL	Handyman	4+2 MU			X
140	XYK 877G	SCAMMELL	Handyman	4+2 MU			
140	770DVW	SCAMMELL	Highwayman	4+2 MU			X
141	924CVW	SCAMMELL	Highwayman	4+2 MU			
141	WYX 682 G	SCAMMELL	Handyman	4+2 MU			X
142	86XNO	SCAMMELL	Highwayman	4+2 MU	Caxton		X
142	921CVW	BEDFORD	S TYPE	4+2 MU			
143	207CVX	BEDFORD	S TYPE	4+2 MU			
143	KVX 469C	ATKINSON	borderer	6+4 Tank			X
143	GMF 350N	VOLVO	F88	4+2 MU			
144	WYX 705G	SCAMMELL	Handyman	4+2 MU			
144	208CVX	SCAMMELL	Highwayman	4+2 MU			
144	GMH 497N	VOLVO	F88	4+2 MU			X

Crow Carrying Co Ltd Fleet List 145-167

leet	Reg plate	Truck name 1	Truck name 2	Truck type	Contract	Driver	Photo
145	GMH 907N	VOLVO	F88	4+2 MU			
145	353EVW	BEDFORD	S TYPE	4+2 Tank			
146	AYM 140H	SCAMMELL	Handyman	4+2 MU	YHS		X
146	354EVW	BEDFORD	S TYPE	4+2 Tank			
146	VOO964	AEC	Mercury	4+2 Tank			X
147	WYX 653G	SCAMMELL	Handyman	4+2 MU			
147	355EVW	BEDFORD	S TYPE	4+2 MU		Phil Hartwell	X
148		SCAMMELL	Handyman	4+2 MU			
148	858GPU	SCAMMELL	Highwayman	4+2 MU			
149	705VOO	AEC	Mercury	4+2 Tank			
149	178PHK	BEDFORD	A5	4+2 Tank			
150	MLW 677D	SCAMMELL	Highwayman	4+2 MU			X
150	179FHK	BEDFORD	A5	4+2 Tank			X
151	GJD 352D	BEDFORD	TK	4+2 MU			
151	690FPV	BEDFORD	S TYPE	4+2 MU			
151	VYK 477M	VOLVO	F86	4+2 MU			X
152	211FVX	BEDFORD	S TYPE	4+2 MU		Ray Oliff	X
153		AEC	Mandator	4+2 MU			
153	212FVX	BEDFORD	S TYPE	4+2 MU	Hercules		X
154	213FVX	BEDFORD	A5	4+2 Tank			
154	KGH 741K	VOLVO	F88	4+2 MU			
155	661HNO	SCAMMELL	Highwayman	4+2 MU	Geigy		X
155	AYN 213H	SCAMMELL	Handyman	4+2 MU			
156		AEC		4+2 Tank			
156	174HVX	BEDFORD	A5	4+2 Tank			
156	VYN 492M	VOLVO	F86	4+2 MU			
157	175HVX	BEDFORD	A5	4+2 Tank			X
157	WYM 710G	SCAMMELL	Handyman	4+2 Tank			
158	176HVX	BEDFORD	A5	4+2 Tank			
158	949F	SCAMMELL	Highwayman	4+2 MU			
159	XBY 858G	AEC	Mandator	4+2 MU			
159	177HVX	BEDFORD	A5	4+2 Tank			
160	UMX 108F	AEC	Mandator	4+2 MU			X
160	178HVX	BEDFORD	A5	4+2 Tank			
161	SGP 52F	AEC	Mandator	4+2 MU			X
161	179HVX	AEC	Mercury	4+2 Tank			
162	180HVX	SCAMMELL	Highwayman	4+2 MU			X
163	181HVX	SCAMMELL	Highwayman	4+2 MU			X
164	FLK768J	SCANIA	110	4+2 MU			
164	973CVW						
165		VOLVO	F86	4+2 MU		Terry Edwards	X
165	192JHK	BMC		4+2 Tank			
166	193JHK	BMC		4+2 Tank			
167	RUL 948E	AEC	Mandator	4+2 MU			X
167	292JHK	ALBION		4+2 MU			X

Crow Carrying Co Ltd Fleet List 168-192

leet	Reg plate	Truck name 1	Truck name 2	Truck type	Contract	Driver	Photo
168	RYP 778E	BEDFORD	TK	4+2 MU	Hercules		X
168	293JHK	ALBION		4+2 MU			X
169	AVF 471H	BMC		4+2 Tank			
169	AVW 796B	BEDFORD	TK	4+2 MU			
170	AVW52F	AEC	Mercury	4+2 MU			
170	AYN 212H	SCAMMELL	Handyman	4+2 MU			
170	1525F	AEC	Mercury	4+2 Tank			X
171	AYN 214H	SCAMMELL	Handyman	4+2 MU			X
171	1526F	SCAMMELL	Highwayman	4+2 MU	Geigy		X
172	4094HK	SCAMMELL	Highwayman	4+2 MU			X
173	4095HK	SCAMMELL	Highwayman	4+2 MU			X
174	8164F	SCAMMELL	Highwayman	4+2 MU			X
174	KGH 742K	SCANIA	110	4+2 MU		Harry Fowler	X
175	HVW 949C	COMMER	TS3	4+2 MU			
175	8263F	AUSTIN		4+2 Tank			
176	GJD 353D	BEDFORD	TK	4+2 MU			X
176	8165F	AUSTIN		4+2 Tank			
176	OLP101L	VOLVO	F86	4+2 MU			
177	WYX 706G	SCAMMELL	Handyman	4+2 MU			
177	6511HK	SCAMMELL	Highwayman	4+2 MU			
178	6512HK	SCAMMELL	Highwayman	4+2 MU			X
178	192FHK	BEDFORD	S TYPE	4+2 Tank			
179	6513HK	SCAMMELL	Highwayman	4+2 MU		Tom Ashworth	X
180	VMX 108F	AEC	Mandator	4+2 MU			
180	6514HK	SCAMMELL	Highwayman	4+2 MU	Thomas Hedley		X
181	428CKX	ATKINSON		8+4 Tank			
182	OLP102L	VOLVO	F86	4+2 MU			X
182	RYP 775E	BEDFORD	TK	4+2 MU			
183		SCAMMELL	Highwayman	4+2 MU			
183	6371TW	AEC	Mercury	4+2 Tank			X
183	OLC 414L	VOLVO	F86	4+2 MU			X
184	OLC 415L	VOLVO	F86	4+2 MU			X
184	5724VX	AEC	Mercury	4+2 Tank			X
185	OWC94	SCAMMELL	Highwayman	4+2 MU			
186	WYK 692G	SCAMMELL	Handyman	4+2 MU			
187	WYK 690G	SCAMMELL	Handyman	4+2 MU			X
187	5725VX	BEDFORD	TJ	4+2 Tank			X
188	5726VX	BEDFORD	TJ	4+2 Tank			
188		SCAMMELL	Handyman	4+2 MU			X
189	3584PU	ATKINSON	borderer	8+4 Tank			
189	AYF 470H	BMC	Mastiff	4+2 Tank			X
190	AYN 215H	BMC	Mastiff	4+2 Tank			X
191	WYK 685G	SCAMMELL	Handyman	4+2 MU			X
191	3586PU	SCAMMELL	Routeman	8+4 Tank			
192	3587PU	SCAMMELL	Highwayman	4+2 MU			

Crow Carrying Co Ltd Fleet List 193-234

leet	Reg plate	Truck name 1	Truck name 2	Truck type	Contract	Driver	Photo
193	3588PU	BEDFORD	S TYPE	4+2 MU			
193	RYK 950E	GUY	Big J	4+2 MU			X
194	3589PU	SCAMMELL	Highwayman	4+2 MU			
195	7376PU	BEDFORD	TJ	4+2 MU	Hercules		X
196	750VPU	SCAMMELL	Highwayman	4+2 MU			
197	751UPU	SCAMMELL	Highwayman	4+2 MU			X
197	NMR 310N	ATKINSON	borderer	4+2 MU			
198							
199	753VPU	SCAMMELL	Highwayman	4+2 MU			
200	754VPU	SCAMMELL	Highwayman	4+2 MU			
201	755VPU						
202	JMC28N	ATKINSON	borderer	4+2 MU			
202		LEYLAND	Comet	4+2 MU	P.R Chemicals		X
203	809UVX	LEYLAND	Comet	4+2 MU			
204	899UVX						
204	WYX 704G	SCAMMELL	Handyman	4+2 MU	Hercules		X
205							
206	FLC 777J	LEYLAND	Boxer	4+2 MU			
206	811YHK	SCAMMELL	Highwayman	4+2 MU			
206		LEYLAND	Boxer	4+2 MU			
207	143DVX	BEDFORD	S TYPE	4+2 Tank			
208							
209	FLK 282G	BMC		4+2 MU			
209	C007781	LEYLAND	Comet	4+2 MU			
210	FLK 283G	BMC		4+2 MU			
210	OO4399	AEC	Mercury	4+2 Tank			
211	EOO599	AEC	Mercury	4+2 Tank			X
212	OO9834	AEC	Mercury	4+2 Tank			
213	OWC745	SCAMMELL	Highwayman	4+2 MU			
214	XWC275	SCAMMELL	Highwayman	4+2 MU			
215	OCL 423L	LEYLAND	Boxer	4+2 MU			X
215	OWC47	SCAMMELL	Highwayman	4+2 MU			
216	XWC280						
217	BHK 903B	AEC	Mercury	4+2 Tank			X
217		SCAMMELL	Highwayman	4+2 MU			X
218	OWC948	ATKINSON	Silver Night	4+2 MU			
218	NMR 197N	ERF	A Series	4+2 MU			
219	KVX 468C	BEDFORD	TK	4+2 MU			X
220	LVC193	SCAMMELL	Highwayman	4+2 MU			
221	AVW 797B	ATKINSON	borderer	8+4 Tank			X
221	OMC 377L	GUY	Big J	4+2 Tank			
222	BPU 134B	SCAMMELL	Highwayman	4+2 MU			
223		SCAMMELL	Highwayman	4+2 MU			X
223	OMC 378L	GUY	Big J	4+2 MU			
224	WYX 702G	SCAMMELL	Handyman	4+2 MU			

Crow Carrying Co Ltd Fleet List 230-262

leet	Reg plate	Truck name 1	Truck name 2	Truck type	Contract	Driver	Photo
225	DOO 415B	SCAMMELL	Highwayman	4+2 MU			
226	DOO 416B	SCAMMELL	Highwayman	4+2 MU			
226	OMC 380L	GUY	Big J	4+2 MU			
227							
228	JEV 764C	BEDFORD	TJ	4+2 MU			X
229							
230							
231	FWC 821B	SCAMMELL	Highwayman	4+2 MU			
231	OMC 381L	GUY	Big J	4+2 MU			
232	MUM 196D						
232	GMK 816M	ERF	A Series	4+2 MU			
233	MGY 214D	SCAMMELL	Highwayman	4+2 MU			X
234	OMC 375L	ERF	A Series	4+2 MU			X
234	MYT99D	BEDFORD	TK	4+2 MU			
234	WYM 702G	SCAMMELL	Handyman	4+2 MU			
235	BMB 439K	ERF	A Series	4+2 MU			X
235	GJD 354J	BEDFORD	TK	4+2 MU			X
236	GJD 355J	GUY	Big J	4+2 MU			
236	OMC 376L	ERF	A Series	4+2 MU			
237	GJD 356J	SCAMMELL	Highwayman	4+2 MU			X
237	UMC 605M	ERF	A Series	4+2 MU			X
238	GJD 357J	SCAMMELL	Highwayman	4+2 MU			
238	TMT 349M	ERF	A Series	4+2 MU			
239	RYU 956E	GUY	Big J	4+2 MU			
240	SGC 444F	LEYLAND		4+2 MU			
240	VYP 417M	ERF	A Series	4+2 MU			
241	XBY 857G	SCAMMELL	Handyman	4+2 MU			X
241	HMN 506M	ERF	A Series	4+2 MU			
242	XBY 860G	SCAMMELL	Handyman	4+2 MU			X
243	XBY 862G	SCAMMELL	Handyman	4+2 MU			X
244	MBY 162D						
245	WYX 688G	AEC	Mandator	4+2 MU			
246							
247	XGX 674G	AEC	Mercury	4+2 MU			
248	XGO 200G	SCAMMELL	Handyman	4+2 MU			
249	XGO 201G	SCAMMELL	Handyman	4+2 MU			
262	NHK13L	SCAMMELL	Trunker	6+2MU	Gramos Chemicals		X

Crow Carrying Co Ltd Fleet List Northern Division

CROW CARRYING (NORTHERN)

ATKINSON BORDERER 4X2 MU

FL.NO	REG.NO	YEAR	DT PURCHASED
C.50	OLC410L	1972	00.11.75
C.51	OLC419L	1972	00.11.75
C.34	OLC420L	1972	00.11.75
C.80	THT483M	1973	00.11.75
C.197	NMR310N	1975	00.11.75
C.202	JMC38N	1975	00.11.75

BMC   4X2 TANK

FL.NO	REG.NO	YEAR	DT PURCHASED
C190	AYH215H	1970	00.11.75

ERF A SERIES   4X2 MU

FL.NO	REG.NO	YEAR	DT PURCHASED
C235	BMB435K	1972	00.11.75
C234	OMC375L	1973	00.11.75
C236	OMC376L	1973	00.11.75
C238	TMT349M	1973	00.11.75
C120	TMT484M	1973	00.11.75
C240	VYP417M	1974	00.11.75
C232	GMK816M	1974	00.11.75
C241	HMN509M	1975	00.11.75
C218	NMR197N	1975	00.11.75
		1974	

ERF B SERIES   4X2 MU

FL.NO	REG.NO	YEAR	DT PURCHASED
CN01	LJP972P	1976	00.01.76
CN02	LJP973P	1976	00.01.76
CN03	NDJ301P	1976	00.01.76
CN04	NBD651P	1976	00.01.76
CN05	OBD72R	1976	00.01.76
CN06	OBK546R	1976	00.01.76
CN07	PJP360R	1976	00.10.76
CN08	RKN322R	1977	00.03.77
CN09	REK503R	1977	00.03.77
CN10	RJP321R	1977	00.04.77

GUY BIG J4T   4X2 MU

FL.NO	REG.NO	YEAR	DT PURCHASED
C221	OMC377L	1973	00.11.75
C223	OMC378L	1973	00.11.75
C226	OMC380L	1973	00.11.75
C231	OMC381L	1973	00.11.75

VOLVO F88-F86

FL.NO	REG.NO	YEAR	DT PURCHASED
C183	OLC414L	1972	00.11.75
C185	OLC416L	1972	00.11.75
C103	UMG580M	1973	00.11.75
C64	UMG593M	1973	00.11.75
C156	VYA492M	1974	00.11.75
C143	GMF350N	1974	00.11.75
C144	GMH497N	1974	00.11.75
C145	GMH907N	1974	00.11.75

SCAMMELL HANDYMAN III   4X2 MU

FL.NO	REG.NO	YEAR	DT PURCHASED
C45	XYK879G	1968	00.11.75
C224	WYX702G	1968	00.11.75
C47	XGO198G	1968	00.11.75
C38	WYX694G	1969	00.11.75
C99	WYX709G	1969	00.11.75
C140	XYK877G	1969	00.11.75
C132	AYN210H	1970	00.11.75
C155	AYN213H	1970	00.11.75
C171	AYN214H	1970	00.11.75

MAGIRUS DEUTZ

FL.NO	REG.NO	YEAR	DT PURCHASED
CN11	SED512R	1977	00.06.77
CN12	SED462R	1977	00.06.77
CN13	TJP461S	1977	00.06.77
CN14	UDJ172S	1977	00.09.77
CN15	UED711S	1977	00.10.77

Crow Carrying Co Ltd - Allocated Fleet List for Trailers Lorries & Drivers from 1980s At Silvertown Depot

FAIL HAZARD TEST   ×

No's Compartments   (2)

1	(0) FLAT	449	(1)		517	(2)	Hurcules	75	496 Searle
60	(2) BVL	450	(1)		518	(3)	Hurcules	77	448 Chapman
220	(2) Petro	460	(1)		1322	(1)	Caustic	78	479 R.Gregory
244	(2) Vinegar	461	(6) Spirit		1425	(1)	Hypo	80	460 N.Gregory
253	(2) Vinegar	462	(6) Spirit		2342	(2)	Hypo	83	502 Stone ADR
254	(2) Vinegar	464	(1)					84	505 Wilkinson ADR
273	(2) Petro	465	(1)					86	374 McKever
322	(1) D storage	467	(1)					89	409 Reeves
328	(1) C E 4 B	468	(1)					90	60 Eammerson
332	(3) Petro	474	(3) L+N					91	253 Battman
334	(5)	475	(1)					94	423 Hartwell
338	(2) Paint	477	(1) (X)					95	467 Stimson
342	(1) Esso	478	(6) Esso					96	468 Lorryman
346	(2) H, L+C	479	(6) Esso					97	351 B.Henry
351	(3) (x)	481	(6) Spirit					99	510 Sutherland ADR
352	(3) fuel Store	482	(6) Spirit					100	450 Williams
359	(5) S,Clean	484	(1) Watling					101	
362	(3) BVL	485	(1)					102	511 R.Walsh ADR
363	(3) Suger	487	(1)					104	509 R.York ADR
374	(2)	488	(1)					105	513 Rudgley ADR
375	(2)	489	(1)					106	504 J.Browning ADR
379	(2)	490	(6) Spirit	38	439		Drisco	108	500 F.Stonhouse
384	(2) (x)	491	(1) ISC	39	465		m.walsh	109	359 P.Thompson
394	(5) Lub oil	492	(1) Bitumen	43	438		Norman	110	464 Dabrille
397	(6) Lub oil	493	(1) Bitumen	44	418		J.Carey	111	220 A.Huish
401	(1) Acid	496	(1)	45	440		Moores	114	512 H.Powell ADR
409	(2) BVL	497	(1)	46	449		Reiley	115	517) Timms
418	(1)	498	(1)	47	497		Liddard		518) Timms
421	(2)	499	(1)	49	498		Barnfiled		
422	(2)	500	(1)	51					
423	(1)	502	(1) ADR	52					
426	(2)	503	(0) Container	54	477		Pennington		
428	(2) Watlington	504	(3) ADR	57	487				
431	(2) M.V	505	(3) ADR	58	422		Howard		
433	(2)	506	(1) Bitumen	59	384		Middleton		
435	(1) Watlington	507	(1) Bitumen	60	426		Newman		
438	(1) H, P.G	508	(1) Bitumen	62	499		M.		
439	(1)	509	(3) ADR	64	447		Seward		
440	(1)	510	(3) ADR	67	489		Lee		
443	(2)	511	(3) ADR	68	478		Snooks		
444	(1) (x)	512	(3) ADR	69	375		V.wood		
447	(2) L+N	513	(1) ADR	72	474		Lythal		
448	(2) L+N	514	(6) Spirit	73	379		Appleton		
		516	(6) Spirit	74	475		Charnick		

Crow Carrying Co Ltd - Drivers List 1920 -1985

	TRUCK	NAME	NIC NAME	YEAR STARTED	Contracts
1.	38)	DENNY .DRISCO			
2.	39	M.WALSH			
3.	43	NORMAN			
4.	44	JOHN.CAREY			
5.	45	MOORES			
6.	46	HENRY.REILEY		24-5-54	
7.	47	ALFRED.LIDDARD		24-10-60	
8.	49	JACKIE.BARNFIELD			
9.	54	TOMMY .PENNINGTON			
10.	58	HOWDD			
11.	59	MIDDLETON			
12.	60	NEWMAN			
13.	62	MCLALEN			
14.	64	SEWALD			
15.	67	J.LEE			
16.	68	JOHNNY.SNOOKS		11-8-70	
17.	69	V.WOOD			
18.	72	LARRY.LYHAL	BUBBLES		
19.	73	APPLETON			
20.	74	CHESUICK			
21.	75	SEARLE			
22.	77	CHAPMAN			
23.	78	R.GREGORY			
24.	80	N.GREGORY			
25.	83	A.STONE		29-6-64	
26.	84	A.WILKINS	JOE THE CROW	29-5-63	
27.	86	MCKEVER			
28.	89	REEVES			
29.	90	EAMELSON			
30.	91	TEDDY.BATTMAN		12-4-55	
31.	94	PHIL.HARTWELL			
32.	95	STEMPSON			
33.	96	J. LORRYMAN		15-1-68	
34.	97	B.HENRY			
35.	99	ERNIE.SUTHERLAND		21-10-68	
36.	100	WILLIAMS			
37.	102	ROGER.WALSH	THE DODGER	13-9-65	
38.	104	ROBERT.YORK	YORKIE	4-11-64	
39.	105	LES.RUGLEY		21-10-68	
40.	106	JACK.BROWNING	HANDSOME JACK	26-2-62	
41.	108	FRED.STONEHOUSE			
42.	109	P.THOMPSON			
43.	110	JOHNNY.DABRILLA			
44.	111	ALLEN.HUISH			
45.	114	HARRY.POWELL		7-6-60	
46.	115	TIMMS			

Crow Carrying Co Ltd Drivers List 1920 -1985

No.		Name		Date	
47.		ERIC.MEEKINGS		14-10-60	
48.		D.STEWART		6-5-57	
49.		A.HARRIS		15-6-62	
50.		GEORGE.LIDDARD		28-1-63	
51.		L.BRAND		16-9-63	
52.		T.HOULAHAN		20-11-64	
53.		A.FOWLER		25-6-65	
54.		WILLIAM.HUMPHREYS		20-9-65	
55.		TERRY.EDWARDS		11-10-65	
56.		K.GREGORY		15-4-66	
57.		JOE.CURTIS		18-7-66	
58.		J.SOUTAR		24-3-69	
59.		ALLEN.GREEN		9-3-70	
60.		W.CONWAY		1-6-71	
61.		TOMMY.LUCAS		21-6-71	
62.		B.PEARSON		6-9-71	
63.		J.COURT		2-11-71	
64.		IAN.YORK		MID 60S	
65.		A.HARDING	SNOWY		
66.		TONY.KING		1957	
67.		MC CORMACK	MACK		DROVE 127 SCAMMELL SHOWBOAT
68.		JACK THRESHIE		1930	50 YEARS IN SERVICE
69.		TONY.WHITE			
70.		JACK. KNIGHTINGGALE			
71.		R.ROWE			
72.		JIMMY.PREIST			
73.		CHARLIE.HAWKSBEE		1948&1963	
74.		D.FRANIS			
75.		J.WILKSHIRE			
76.		B.WALLER			
77.		H.WALLER			
78.		J.MATTHEWS		1940S	
79.		JOHN.SMITH		15-5-51	
80.		GUS.GASCOIN		1960	
81.		J.COLLINS			
82.		TOMMY.CRAWFORD			
83.		RAY.OLIFF		1958	
84.		ALBERT.SMITH			
85.		GEORGE.ROBINSON			
86.		BRIAN PEARSON			
87.	161	TOM LORD			
88.	52	ALBERT HARRIS			
89.	43	BILL MOORS			
90.	74	BRIAN WYDER			
91.		RICHARD BAILEY			

1980s Staff at Crow Carrying Co Ltd in Silvertown

CROW MANAGERS

Peter Reeves   Managing Director

Keith Clarke   Financial Director

Ron Ansell   Fleet Engineer, when he left his position was taken by Jeff Braithwaite

Leon Cogdale   Transport Manager, when he left his position was taken by Chris Shoesmith

Ron Hammond   Traffic operator

WORKSHOP STAFF

George Huchison   Garage Foreman

Barry Sciven   Stores Manager

Nobby Clarke   Stores clerk (no relation to Keith)

Colin Butcher   Fitter

Alf Butcher   Fitter/welder (colins dad)

David Turner   Fitter (now service manager at the Scania dealer in Purfleet)

Len Mulley   Painter/signwriter

Joseph Camillerri   Painter

Bashir Ahmed   Fitter

M. Solanki   Fitter

Crow Carrying Co Ltd
Letter Heads through the Years

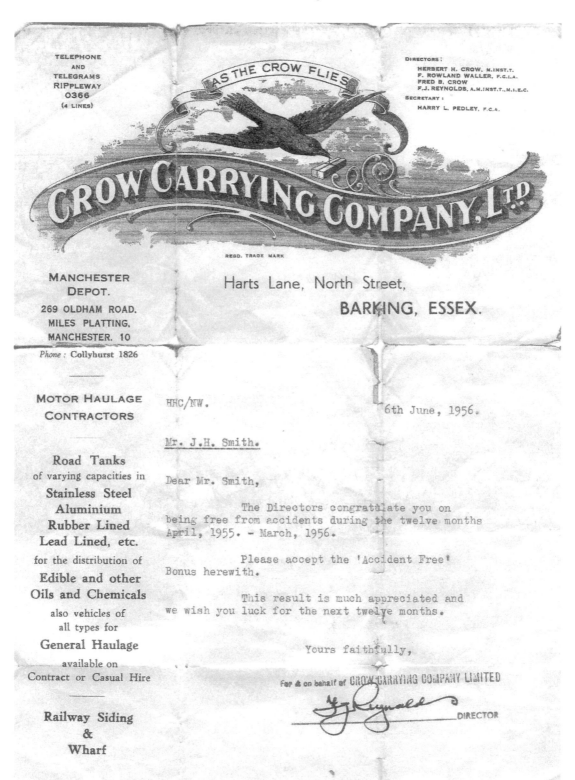

Crow Carrying Co Ltd
Letter Heads through the Years

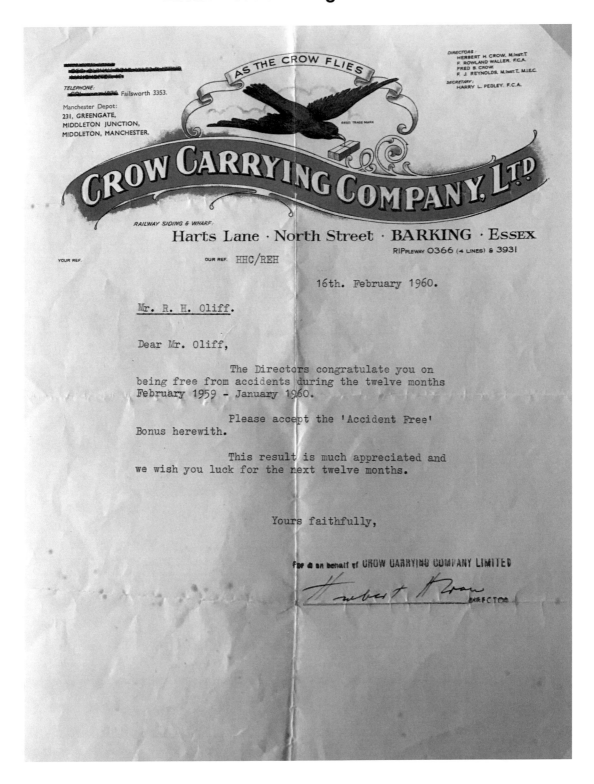

Crow Carrying Co Ltd
Letter Heads through the Years

DEPOTS: Hedon Road, Hull HU9 5PL   Tel.: 0482 702274/5
Upton Lane, Nursling, Southampton SO1 9XY   Tel.: 0703 736011/2

Directors: J. B. Duncan P. J. Reeves (Managing) J. J. D. Braithwaite J. Wishart

Crow Carrying Company Ltd.

Reg. Office
**NORTH WOOLWICH ROAD
LONDON E16 2BG**
Reg. No. 168224 (England)
Telephone: 01-476 0211 (10 lines)
Telex: 896529

Crow Time Sheet

Time Sheets

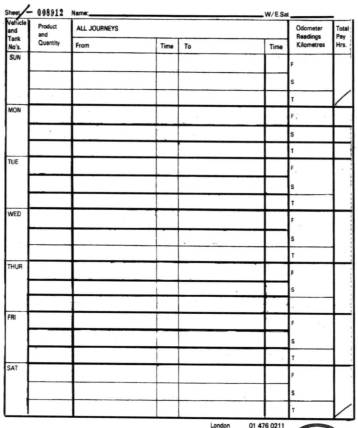

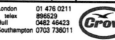

The End of Crow Carrying Co Ltd - 1985

In 1960s Crow Carrying Company, were eventually taken over by TDG, but still continued to run and operate in its own name.

In 1970 they had a 250 strong fleet. In 1985 TDG merged with Reliance Tankers from Sale in Manchester. Not long after this they created the first Linkman brand.

Another name in Crow's transition were Buckley Tankers, all under the TDG banner. Then it became TDG in its own right. TDG were eventually taken over in 2011 by Norbert Dentressangle, finally in 2015 by XPO from USA. So the spirit of Crow's definitely lives on but not in name.

Crow Carrying Co l.t.d

Magnificent Seven

C. York

1964 - 1985

....

1950s
Stores - Electrical workshop staff
Leon Cogdale - Dave Doe - George Paramore - John Denyer - Jock brice - Bill Bunik
Bob Paine - Nobby Clark - George Austin - Jim Denyer - Alf Martin
Paint Shop & Metal Workshop staff
Jim Fletche - Lenny Mully -Bill Tiller - Van Veen - John Airs - Frank Frances

Crow Carrying Co Logo's & Signs through the Years

Crow Carrying
Company Ltd.
London E16 2BG

Acknowledgements

Arthur Imgram - Peter Davies -Commercial Motor - Jack Threshie - Alfred Liddard - Terry Edwards
George Robinson - Jerry Hayes - Tony King - Lenny Mulley's Wife - Johnny Caygill - Roger Walsh -
Billy Golding - Tom Lord & Son - Richard Scrivens - Jackie Barnfield
Tommy Pennington - Larry Lythall - Kenny Charnick - Jack Browning - George Liddard
Alfred Fowler - William Humphreys - Tommy Lucas - Ian York - Robert York - Jimmy Preist
Charlie Hawksbee - Gus Gascoin - Ray Oliff - Alf Tucker - Ron Hammond - Fred Stonehouse
Darren Fowler - George Paramore - Cliff Stimpson - Micky Walsh - Kevin Tabram
Bill Wheeler's Son - James Matthews - John Smith - Henry Reilly - Brian Smith - Philip Hartwell -
Alexander Wilkins - Joe Curtis - Les Rudgley - Ernest Sutherland - Jimmy Lorryman & Son
Brian Wylde - Richard Bailey - Michael Mckever - Johnny Dabbrilla - Alan Huish - Eric Meekings
Mick Hall - Allen Green - Robert Pope -NAT3 Photos - Vintage Commercial Vehicles Magazine
& Vintage Roadsene Magazine for there contribution.
and Marion Goodyear & Dave Young & my sister Teresa Fletcher for all there help
Finally a special thanks to Peter Sumpter for his encouragement.
Carol Cooper (Proof Reader) from the Scammell club

That was the Crow Carrying Company story from 1920 to 1985
In conclusion I trust this illustrated
account of the growth and activities of Crow Carrying Company Ltd and those
who worked there over 65 years has been of interest to you.

Clinton York

Lightning Source UK Ltd.
Milton Keynes UK
UKRC012259270119
336312UK00016B/407